Great Tastes

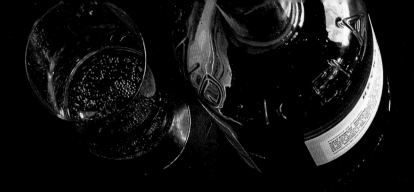

DANIELLE & LAURA KOSANN

GREAT

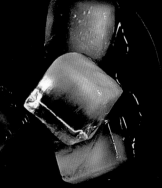

Clarkson Potter/Publishers
New York

TASTES

COOKING (AND EATING) FROM MORNING TO MIDNIGHT

FOREWORD BY CHRISTINA TOSI

Photographs by Aubrie Pick

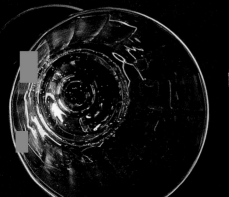

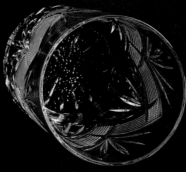

For all the potatoheads out there, thank you for inspiring us every day. This book is for you.

CONTENTS

IF YOU ASK ME, THE SECRET TO LIFE IS CELEBRATING, INDULGING IN, REMAINING PASSIONATELY CURIOUS.

When I first met Danielle and Laura, they had just launched The New Potato, interviewing my pal and restaurateur Gabe Stulman.

Though it's hard to take a man like that away from his dining room, Danielle and Laura cared less about what the celebrated guy *served* and more about what made him *tick*. What fueled his creative spirit when designing restaurants? They only asked questions worthy of a best friend chatting over a nightcap at midnight. It was such a human approach, yet so off the beaten path. Their curiosity was their hook. Both in getting Gabe to agree to the interview and in piquing our curiosity.

Not too long after, the two asked me to lend my Upper West Side Milk Bar to a shoot they planned with supermodel Karlie Kloss. What business did a supermodel have in a bakery? Was this a joke? I was curious. Turns out the joke was on me. What does a gal whose job is to look good indulge in? What are her secrets to keeping it fresh when she's living on an airplane? Whose closet of clothes does she admire most? We bonded over cookies, blue jeans, and the nostalgia of the Midwest—we became fast friends for life.

Danielle and Laura are tastemakers in and of themselves. I've watched these two humble, hella hip, multifaceted, talented women work and it's awe-inspiring. They connect and bond with people through the lens in which they see the world on a much deeper level than the all-too-obvious surface. They understand what we really want and what we really need. Our voyeuristic desire to connect, to be let in on secrets, to discover the unexpected in someone, was their hook.

But what came next is truly their craft. The curiosity they share with the world creates a jungle gym of ideas and inspiration to carry through life. They break down walls, they curate, and they redefine what and who is the authority on food, fashion, travel, beauty, entertainment, and everything in between. They have an untouchable, undefinable, unimpeachable, unstoppable magical touch, that makes the world feel like your very own playground. They demand that crushing life on your terms is not about being intimidated, it's about embracing. Creating a level of taste all one's own. It's thinking about a true sense of self and a true hospitality beyond conventional definition, about defining food beyond food, creating a sense of time and place, putting a larger weight on connectivity, demanding an emotional response.

What feeds the creative spirit? What fuels the quirk? What nurtures the hustle, the bustle, the push? We've heard from everyone but these two! Danielle and Laura are the new renaissance women where curiosity is king . . . or queen. Curious minds wonder alike, and boy, do they work up an appetite!

—Christina Tosi

WE HAVEN'T FACT-CHECKED THIS, BUT SOMETHING TELLS US WE MAY BE THE ONLY PEOPLE WHO HAVE EVER STARTED A COOKBOOK BY SAYING WE'RE ANTI-FOODIE FOODIES.

Let us back up. Even before we conceived of our website The New Potato in 2012—when Foodie-ism was all the rage—we described ourselves with that term, because it's never *just* been about the food. Rather, food has always permeated every aspect of our lives, but in an accessible and aspirational way, not an intimidating one. We've always believed that food is as much about what surrounds a dish as it is about the dish itself. Whether it's the outfit you wear on date night, the decor of your favorite restaurant, the flowers in the center of the table, or the most perfectly curated dinner party guest list, food is most definitely a 360-degree experience. How can it not be?

Growing up as sisters, we never felt that food was binary. It didn't mean farm to table, or the process behind sous vide–ing, or understanding different types of summer squash. It meant more: family travels and adventures; our mom's somewhat-amateur-yet-delicious honey mustard chicken and rice pilaf; the way our Austrian grandmommy ran around her kitchen in a complete state of organized chaos; the respect and appreciation we had for the look our dad gave us when we started arguing at the table, knowing this was a special meal not to be disrupted; tea and cakes at the Plaza with Nagyi (Hungarian for grandma) while we marveled at the decor; pilfering cheap jewelry from street stands in Little Italy after a family meal at Angelo's, then falling asleep on each other (or fighting over the armrest) in the car ride back to Connecticut. Food permeates every experience and every memory we share. There was never one definition of food, because for us and for our whole family, three meals a day, and what those three meals would look like, were just the anchors.

It was during one of those car rides to Connecticut for the holidays, when we had finally outgrown pushing our elbows against each other for the armrest, that the idea for The New Potato came about.

We'd always thought about doing something together around the idea of food, both of us having a passion for cooking at home and for eating out. The discussion started, though, with a question about what someone like Diane Von Furstenberg or Jenna Lyons has for breakfast every day, or what Jesse Tyler Ferguson serves at a dinner party, or what Lindsey Vonn eats after a workout. Why couldn't you easily find that information somewhere, as you could find their wardrobe choices or vacation spots? The conversation spiraled into why people from all walks of life aren't being asked about food the same way they were being asked about their style, their careers, or their dating status. We couldn't think of a lifestyle destination dedicated to food. "*Vogue* covers the world through a fashion lens, *Vanity Fair* through an entertainment lens, *Rolling Stone* through a music lens. Why isn't there somewhere that covers the world through the lens of what we eat?" we wondered.

Food seemed like the only industry that didn't reach beyond its comfort zone, beyond the typical realm of restaurant openings and recipe exploring. Why weren't actors asked on the Oscars red carpet "what were you eating?" in addition to "who are you wearing?" Did they even want to be asked that?

We decided to build a makeshift website and find out. So we asked. And asked. The New Potato was born from our asking every tastemaker who would talk to us—from an editor in chief like Graydon Carter to an NFL football player like Cameron Newton to an actress like Jessica Alba—the same question: "What would be your ideal food day?" The interview would then lead into many other topics, the idea being that the subject of food made people loosen up. The topic made people comfortable and broke the ice the same way gathering around a course of appetizers and wine does at the start of a dinner party.

The interviews we were able to secure for the website stunned us, as did the enthusiastic response

from the interviewees. Through those first few months, we kept our hopes low for the fashion industry—the only arena we hadn't yet broken into. The fashion set intimidated us; they seemed slightly inaccessible and exclusive. Plus, food didn't seem to be the hottest topic in fashion. . . . What if models gave us answers that food fans found uninteresting? What if top designers picked the people-watching places, not the good-food places? We stuck to our maxim: Everyone has to eat. That means there isn't a right or wrong way to do it.

At first, models, fashion bloggers, and designers alike would have their reps send back responses like "But she isn't an expert on food," "He loves food but he doesn't really cook," and "She doesn't feel that confident talking about the subject." We'd persist and quickly email back, "She doesn't have to be an expert. There are no wrong answers here!"

It didn't take long for the floodgates to open. Not only were the biggest names in fashion some of our most interesting interviews, they were also some of the most interesting on the site overall. From designers like Donna Karan and Zac Posen to models like Karlie Kloss and Chrissy Teigen to actors like Robert De Niro and Diane Kruger to editors in chief like Edward Enninful and Glenda Bailey, the fashion industry completely embraced food. It was as though these people had been itching to talk about the topic forever.

Finally, we had broken the ice in every industry, and we'd done it with our favorite thing in the world.

As The New Potato's identity solidified, we realized more and more that we were unlike any other website, blog, or vertical out there. We didn't review restaurants and we didn't narrate our cooking every day. Instead, we built city guides and recipes based on the material interview subjects gave us. Meeting and talking with them over meals was as important as the meal itself. We were creating an unending stream of experiences and adventures with unbelievable people, all over the subject of food. We began to share our own original content, too, through narrative pieces as well as recipes we loved to make at home.

When the idea of a cookbook started to come up, we laughed and had the same reaction our first few fashion interviewees did: "Who, us? We're not chefs!" Yup. That was the point.

This book is a natural extension of our website—a combination of all its features—because we love food, we love to cook, and we love to eat. Instead of a traditional chapter-by-chapter organization, we've decided to take you through *our* ideal food day—or perhaps several variations on it—from early morning to late at night. And of course, great food is great storytelling, which is why these courses are broken up by funny anecdotes from our lives, both pre–The New Potato and during. These recipes fit into our day-to-day lives while also making that day-to-day a bit more special. They're ambitious but they're still accessible. Most of all, though, they reflect the fact

that our favorite part of food is every part: the act of gathering, the people who pop in and out, the people you bond with over it, the wine you drink while cooking the meal, even the perfect array of tapered candles and flowers you disperse with your sister while your mom dances to bad disco music and watches the oven (sorry, Mom). So this book is as much a collection of hilarious stories from two sisters as it is a smorgasbord of great food. We hope you're hungry!

MORNING

BREAKFAST
(AND BUBBLEGUM IN A DISH)
WITH AUBREY ANDERSON-EMMONS

*W*e thought it would be fun to do a short video in which we go trick-or-treating with a child star—and whether this was a calculated creative decision or a ploy for us to load up on candy as adults is a question we choose not to answer. Our trick-or-treating comrade of choice was the adorable *Aubrey Anderson-Emmons, who plays Lily on* Modern Family.

We were to arrive at Aubrey's house in Los Angeles first thing in the morning. Laura tends to approach every video—even four-minute ones—with a Spielbergian seriousness, so even though trick-or-treating was not the most complex of plotlines, an early start was essential. Danielle emailed Aubrey's mom,

Amy, the night before to get breakfast orders. (You wouldn't want to show up empty-handed, would you?) Aubrey's request was a cinnamon bagel with cream cheese. Easy enough.

The next morning we stood at the bagel shop completely dumbfounded upon seeing both cinnamon-raisin bagels and cinnamon-sugar bagels as options. We were at a loss. Which one had Amy been referring to, and if we messed it up, what would happen? We'd watched enough *Modern Family* to know about the wrath of Lily, and were convinced the actress and character were one and the same.

Our stress might sound ridiculous, but as our mom always said, you only get one chance at making a first impression, and meeting someone under ten is no exception to this rule. Also let's face it, as far as children go, mixing up something like raisins and sugar is the adult equivalent of showing up drunk to a job interview; it's not just frowned upon—it's utterly unacceptable. The stakes were high.

We stood at the counter analyzing Amy's email, as if there were some sort of code to be unlocked from the words "Cinnamon bagel." The man behind the counter eyed us like we were lunatics; even by Los Angeles standards, we were taking an oddly long time to ponder our order.

After debating the matter for a good twenty-three minutes, we went with our gut and decided on cinnamon raisin. We figured we could always say we picked the more nutritious of the two breakfast options in case we had guessed wrong. As this was one of our first video shoots for the website, though, our nerves were making us imagine unreasonable things, like a "No wire hangers!!!!" *Mommie Dearest* scene of sorts—just replace the hangers with a cinnamon-raisin bagel, and Joan Crawford with a four-foot-five seven-year-old. In the end, the catastrophe we'd imagined was avoided. The New Potato and Aubrey Anderson-Emmons became fast friends, thanks to our solid bagel-ordering skills.

While Laura is the younger sister and Danielle the older, the responsible versus irresponsible dynamic you'd usually expect actually sometimes reverses during business matters. Laura's the bad cop, Danielle the good cop. Laura's more type A, Danielle's more type B . . . or C . . . and this video was no exception. While Laura directed people to their positions, made sure everyone was getting mic'd up, and looked over the shots the crew was setting up, Danielle threw herself into her self-assigned task: playing bubblegum bubblegum in a dish with the talent.

The second Laura would say we were starting to shoot, Aubrey would snap into acting mode and abandon the tower of Reese's peanut butter cups she'd built, or the game of rock, paper, scissors she'd been playing. On the other hand, Danielle, the adult, would sit sullenly looking after her like a bored kid one hour into Bring Your Daughter to Work Day.

A few houses into our trick-or-treating mission, Aubrey started to get hungry for lunch. We hurriedly landed on ordering from Chipotle, and while all of the grown-ups opted for complex burrito bowls and salads, Aubrey went minimalist with a cheese quesadilla. We handed our intern John the list of orders and he sped to Chipotle, letting us know via text upon his arrival that there was a forty-five-minute wait. Aubrey said she was hungry a few more times, and we eyed each other nervously realizing there was only one solution: more bubblegum bubblegum in a dish. This time we all joined in and tried to make it as enticing and competitive as Super Bowl Sunday, tapping our fists and counting with as much fervor as Tom Brady himself.

By the time John got back, we'd nearly forgotten about lunch, but Aubrey eagerly took her seat at the table as he unpacked all the bags. We watched him in what seemed like slow motion, as so many boxes came out—but none of them quesadilla shaped. The blood all but drained from our faces. Laura directed John straight back to Chipotle for that cheese quesadilla with the kind of command Moses used to part the Red Sea. Danielle began brainstorming what more she could bring to the table besides a counting game.

Forty minutes later, Danielle was on her tenth variation of the game, Laura was on her tenth call with John, and Aubrey's attention was waning. We were about eleven minutes away from offering to buy her a puppy, when we finally heard John was on his way back, quesadilla in tow.

"If anything happens to that quesadilla . . . I swear . . . John is fired," Laura practically shouted to the video team. It was an empty threat considering John's internship was one day long. Danielle apologized for about the twentieth time to Amy, who told us for the twentieth time there was no need to treat this like the Greek tragedy we were treating it as. After all, at least Aubrey had had a hearty breakfast.

Aubrey gave us a taste of her bagel, and for the record, it was delicious. We love to start our mornings in a hearty way. We never skip breakfast, but we've upgraded cinnamon raisin for cinnamon muesli with dates. Read on for this and a few more of our favorite morning recipes.

CINNAMON MUESLI WITH DATES AND PISTACHIOS

Makes 3 heaping cups

2 cups old-fashioned rolled oats or other rolled cereal

½ cup date pieces or other small dried fruit

½ cup raw pistachios

½ cup hemp hearts

⅓ cup chia seeds

¼ teaspoon ground cinnamon

Small pinch of ground cardamom

1. In a large bowl, combine the oats, fruit, pistachios, hemp hearts, chia seeds, and spices. Transfer the muesli to an airtight container and store in a dark cabinet for up to 1 month.

2. TO SERVE: We like to combine ½ cup muesli with half a grated apple and ¾ cup almond milk (or use the milk of your choice). Let stand at least 15 minutes or refrigerate overnight.

PB&J SMOOTHIE BOWL

Makes 1 bowl

For the smoothie

1 (4-ounce) package frozen açai

1 to 2 tablespoons creamy natural peanut butter

2 tablespoons milk of choice or coconut water

Pinch of kosher salt

For the toppings

3 strawberries, sliced

¼ cup blueberries

¼ cup raspberries

2 tablespoons roasted unsalted peanuts

We're convinced that peanut butter makes everything better—and we still eat PB&J on a regular basis. The flavors in this smoothie bowl are exactly the same (and so, so good), but you're getting way more nutrients than the PB&J from your elementary school days.

1. MAKE THE SMOOTHIE: In a blender, combine the frozen açai, 1 tablespoon of the peanut butter, the milk, and salt. Blend until smooth, then taste and add another tablespoon of peanut butter, if desired.

2. TO SERVE: Pour the smoothie into a bowl and top with the berries and roasted peanuts and enjoy.

GINGERY BANANA BREAD

Makes 1 loaf

½ cup virgin coconut oil, melted, plus
more for greasing

2 tablespoons ground chia seeds
(from about 1 tablespoon whole seeds)

1½ cups spelt flour (or ¾ cup all-purpose
flour plus ¾ cup whole wheat flour)

1 teaspoon baking soda

1 teaspoon ground ginger

¼ teaspoon kosher salt

¾ cup packed coconut sugar or
light brown sugar

1 heaping cup mashed bananas
(from 2 large bananas)

We often have a sweet tooth in the morning, and this banana bread always does the trick. It's the perfect on-the-go breakfast—and makes for a delicious (and nutritious) midmorning snack.

1. Position a rack in the center of the oven and preheat to 325°F. Generously grease an 8½ × 4½-inch metal loaf pan. (You can use a 9 × 5-inch loaf pan, but cut the baking time by 10 to 15 minutes.)

2. In a small bowl, mix the ground chia seeds with ¼ cup plus 2 tablespoons water and let stand until thickened, about 10 minutes.

3. In a large bowl, whisk together the flour, baking soda, ground ginger, and salt. In a medium bowl, whisk together the oil, coconut sugar, mashed bananas, and chia gel. Stir the banana mixture into the dry ingredients until just combined.

4. Scrape the batter into the prepared pan and bake until the loaf is golden and a tester inserted into the center of the loaf comes out clean, 40 to 50 minutes. Let cool in the pan on a wire rack for 15 minutes, then turn the bread out onto the rack to cool completely.

BLUEBERRY-BUCKWHEAT MUFFINS

Makes 1 dozen muffins

4 tablespoons unsalted butter or virgin coconut oil, melted and cooled, plus more for greasing

1 cup all-purpose flour

½ cup buckwheat flour

¼ teaspoon kosher salt

1 teaspoon baking powder

¼ teaspoon baking soda

½ cup packed light brown sugar

1 teaspoon vanilla extract

2 large eggs

1 cup full-fat sour cream or yogurt

1 cup blueberries

These not-too-sweet muffins can be kept at room temperature, covered, for up to 2 days. For the best flavor, halve and rewarm before serving.

1.   Position a rack in the center of the oven and preheat the oven to 375°F. Line or grease a 12-cup muffin tin.

2.   In a large bowl, whisk together the flours, salt, baking powder, and baking soda. In a medium bowl, whisk together the brown sugar, vanilla extract, eggs, sour cream, and melted butter. Stir the wet ingredients into the dry ingredients and fold in the blueberries. Divide the batter evenly among the muffin cups.

3.   Bake the muffins until a tester inserted into the centers comes out clean, 12 to 15 minutes. Let cool for 5 minutes, then transfer the muffins to a rack and let cool completely.

COCONUT-QUINOA PORRIDGE

Serves 4 to 6

For the porridge

1 cup quinoa

2 cups coconut water or regular water

1 (14-ounce) can full-fat coconut milk

2 tablespoons coconut sugar or
light brown sugar

½ teaspoon kosher salt

For the toppings (optional)

Toasted coconut and sliced strawberries

Slivered almonds and sliced peaches

Chopped pistachios and blueberries

Chopped walnuts and diced pears

More sophisticated than oatmeal, but just as easy. You can customize this by adding pinches of sweet spices, like cinnamon or cardamom.

1.   **MAKE THE PORRIDGE:** In a fine-mesh sieve, rinse the quinoa well.

2.   In a medium saucepan, combine the quinoa, coconut water, coconut milk, coconut sugar, and salt and bring to a boil over high heat. Reduce the heat to medium-low and simmer, uncovered, stirring occasionally, until the quinoa is tender and the porridge is thickened, about 20 minutes.

3.   **TO SERVE:** Spoon the quinoa into bowls and serve with toppings, if desired.

THE PUPPY STORE
PROXIMITY EFFECT

*I*t's a fact that establishments serving alcohol should
not be in close proximity to pet stores.

Okay, so it might not be a widely known fact
or something talked about at length or at all, but
trust us that it's definitely a zoning issue for any
walking city. In New York City, to be more specific,
there are pet stores boasting golden retriever
puppies and French bulldogs galore a mere half
block from brunch spots, bars, and happening
downtown restaurants. This simple fact can turn
a young, innocent, and sometimes irresponsible
Manhattanite into a dog owner.

It is known as the Puppy Store Proximity
Effect and Laura is one such Manhattanite.

Laura lived in New York's trendy West Village
just after college and on her walk to work each
day she'd pass Le Petit Puppy, where they display
puppies in the window like stilettos. For a week she
kept seeing the same little black-and-white puppy.

On that particular street, the pet store is the
first thing she'd pass coming from her apartment.
Then a few storefronts later, our two favorite brunch
spots, Jeffrey's Grocery and Joseph Leonard. Those
spots are then followed by Citipups, yet another pet
store with puppies in the window. All in all, this
street is basically a series of morning cocktail and
puppy-purchase land mines.

At Jeffrey's we'd order our favorite dish on
the menu, which is an everything bagel covered in
cream cheese, smoked salmon, capers, tomato, and
red onion; and at Joseph Leonard we'd usually have
avocado toast. On this particular Saturday, avocado
toast, eggs, and Bloody Marys was the order of the

day, and Laura was fifteen minutes late to meet Danielle after ogling that black-and-white dog for the sixth day in a row. Laura's love could not have been purer—there aren't many things that get between us and food.

Danielle was well aware of Laura's new obsession, and thus far had taken on the role of Responsible Older Sister: "We quit our jobs during a recession. We're barely making money trying to get a brand-new website off the ground. Now is not the time to buy a dog."

Laura listened and nodded, hearing only the squawking sounds that emanate from adults in the *Peanuts* movies. Meanwhile the dog's fluffy face and playful gait floated above her, in a thought bubble of yearning.

Danielle had been the only thing keeping this whole puppy scenario from spiraling out of control. But with each sip of Bloody, Danielle began to run lower and lower on ammunition as Laura continued to gush: *His fur ball body, his white snout peppered with black polka dots, his white paws that look like socks . . .*

"Wait. White paws that look like socks? You didn't say anything about white paws that looked like socks," Danielle said.

Oh no.

"Yes!!!!! Paws that look like socks!" Laura said.

Here we go.

"Almost like little mittens?"

Oh crap.

"OMG yes, TOTALLY like mittens."

Eight minutes later, we were outside the pet store, officially in the red zone.

"I just want to see what you think. You have to admit he's cute, right?" Laura asked, as we looked into the window.

Let's be real. The motive behind bringing a disapproving cohort to a pet store to show them a puppy is never to *prove* its cuteness. Unless said cohort is a complete psychopath, she's going to think the puppy is cute. In fact, it's unlikely that anyone has ever concluded that a friend shouldn't get a puppy because its level of adorable is not up to snuff.

Danielle took one more look. "Should we go in and just see how much he is?" She didn't realize that with those words, she'd mapped out the next fifteen or so years of Laura's life. Another eight minutes passed and Laura became a dog owner.

Three days later, Scout was in a crate next to Laura's bed. We wish we could say we learned something, but really all we took away was that boozy brunches can lead to unconditional, tail-wagging love. Oh, and Danielle now has a brunch-fueled puppy as well. What can we say? Responsible decisions may come and go, but a good Bloody Mary is forever.

Brunch is more of a time to splurge (and we don't mean on puppies). The following recipes are some of our favorites.

LIME-BLUEBERRY PANCAKES

Makes about 15 pancakes

1½ cups all-purpose flour

2 teaspoons baking powder

½ teaspoon baking soda

½ teaspoon kosher salt

1½ cups buttermilk

2 large eggs

2 tablespoons pure maple syrup,
plus more for serving

2 teaspoons vanilla extract

Grated zest of 2 limes

6 tablespoons virgin coconut oil
(see Note) or unsalted butter,
melted, plus more for the pan

1½ cups blueberries

NOTE: *We prefer virgin coconut oil for the flavor it adds, but you can use regular as well.*

Aside from these being perfect, fluffy blueberry pancakes, the lime zest adds a whole other dimension to them. And, if you like, you can even make lime maple syrup. For every 2 tablespoons syrup, whisk in ½ teaspoon lime juice. Voilà!

1. Preheat the oven to 225°F and set a baking sheet in the oven.

2. In a large bowl, whisk together the flour, baking powder, baking soda, and salt. In a small bowl, whisk together the buttermilk, eggs, syrup, vanilla, lime zest, and melted coconut oil.

3. Heat a nonstick skillet or a griddle over medium heat until hot. Lightly oil the surface with coconut oil. Add the liquid ingredients to the dry ingredients and stir together until just combined, with a few lumps remaining. Fold in the blueberries.

4. For each pancake, scoop about 3 tablespoons of the batter into the skillet. Cook until the bottoms are golden, bubbles form on top, and the pancakes look dry around the edges, about 3 minutes. Flip the pancakes and cook until just cooked through, 1 to 2 minutes longer. Reduce the heat if the pancakes start to get too brown. Transfer the pancakes to the oven to keep warm and repeat with the remaining batter.

5. Serve the pancakes with more maple syrup alongside.

EGG-AVOCADO SANDWICH WITH SPICY MAYO

Makes 4 sandwiches

4 English muffins, split and toasted
(or 8 slices bread, toasted)

¼ cup mayonnaise

2 teaspoons Sriracha sauce

½ cup arugula

1 Hass avocado, halved and sliced

4 red radishes, thinly sliced

½ tablespoon unsalted butter

4 large eggs

Kosher salt and freshly ground pepper

Without fail, if we make an egg sandwich at home, we are piling on the Sriracha. One day we decided we needed an upgrade, and this spicy mayo was born. We love this sandwich on an English muffin, but it's equally delicious on gluten-free or sprouted-grain bread if you're looking for a more nutritious alternative.

1. Arrange the toasted muffins cut side up on a work surface.

2. In a small bowl, mix together the mayonnaise and Sriracha. Slather the cut sides of the muffins with the mayo mixture.

3. Divide the arugula among the bottom halves of the muffins. Arrange the avocado and radish slices on the top half of the muffins.

4. In a nonstick skillet or on a griddle, melt the butter over medium heat. Crack the eggs (working in batches if needed) into the skillet, and using the corner of the spatula, break the yolk. Cook, turning once, until the eggs are just set, 2 to 3 minutes.

5. Season the eggs with salt and pepper and transfer to the bottom sides of the muffins. Close the sandwiches and serve.

GOAT CHEESE AND MUSHROOM SCRAMBLE

Serves 4

3 tablespoons unsalted butter

½ pound mixed mushrooms,
cut into bite-size pieces

Kosher salt

1 medium shallot, finely chopped

8 large eggs

Freshly ground pepper

2 ounces goat cheese, crumbled

1 tablespoon thinly sliced chives,
plus more for garnish

This recipe wouldn't exist without Danielle's husband, Seth, who makes a mean scrambled egg. This recipe showcases one of his favorite combos. The key here is to cook the mushrooms and shallots first.

1. In a large nonstick skillet, melt 2 tablespoons of the butter over medium-high heat. When the foam subsides, add the mushrooms and a large pinch of salt and cook, stirring frequently, until the mushrooms are softened and browned, about 8 minutes. Reduce the heat to medium and melt the remaining butter. Add the shallot and cook until softened, 1 to 2 minutes.

2. In a bowl, whisk the eggs with 1 tablespoon water and season with salt and pepper. Add the eggs to the skillet. Cook, stirring frequently, until the eggs are nearly set but still slightly loose, about 2 minutes. Remove the skillet from the heat and sprinkle the eggs with the goat cheese and the chives. Return the skillet to medium heat and cook, stirring, until the eggs are cooked to your liking. Transfer the eggs to plates, garnish with chives, and serve hot.

SMOKED SALMON EGGS BENEDICT WITH POTATO PANCAKES AND AVOCADO HOLLANDAISE

Serves 4

8 large eggs

Lemon-Dill Mashed Potato Cakes (page 180)

8 ounces thinly sliced smoked salmon

Avocado Hollandaise (recipe follows)

Chopped dill, for garnish

NOTE: *To rewarm already poached eggs, fill a clean pot with water and heat until very warm. Submerge the eggs in the water for about 1 minute, then use a slotted spoon to remove them from the water.*

Yes, we know—eggs and avocado again. But, quite honestly, it's a match made in heaven. Because there are several components to this recipe, it might seem daunting, but you can make many of the components ahead of time. For instance, you can make and cook the potato pancakes a day ahead and rewarm them in a skillet (or just prepare the mixture ahead and fry them fresh). The avocado hollandaise can be made up to 6 hours in advance. And believe it or not, you can poach eggs a day ahead and refrigerate them in cold water; just reheat them in warm water before serving (see Note).

1. Bring a large pot of water to a very slight simmer over medium heat (reduce the heat as needed to maintain the slight simmer). Arrange paper towels on a plate and place nearby. Crack 1 egg into a fine-mesh strainer set over a bowl and shake gently to remove the excess liquid. Transfer the egg to a small bowl or ramekin. Repeat with a second egg, placing it in a separate bowl.

2. Stir the pot of water to create a vortex, then quickly slip in the 2 eggs, one egg at a time, and poach until the whites are opaque throughout and the yolks are still runny, about 3 minutes. Using a slotted spoon, transfer the eggs to the paper towels. Repeat the process with the remaining eggs until you have poached all the eggs. (If you feel comfortable, you can poach more than 2 eggs at a time. If you're working ahead, transfer the poached eggs to a bowl of ice water and refrigerate overnight.)

3. To assemble the Benedicts, divide the potato cakes among four plates. Top with the smoked salmon, followed by the poached eggs. Drizzle each with the hollandaise, garnish with dill, and serve.

Avocado Hollandaise

Makes about 2 cups

2 small Hass avocados

2 tablespoons fresh
lemon juice

¼ cup extra-virgin olive oil

Kosher salt

In a blender, combine the avocados, lemon juice, and ¾ cup water and pulse until the avocado is finely chopped. Blend for 1 to 2 minutes to puree, scraping down the sides as needed. With the motor running, stream in the olive oil. Season with salt. If making ahead, store in an airtight container in the refrigerator.

MIDDAY

AN AMERICAN
(AND HER SISTER)
IN PARIS

*W*hen Laura studied abroad in Paris for a semester in college, her "look" evolved into a sort of mix between Geppetto, the woodcarver from Pinocchio, and a chorus girl from Les Misérables. *Our mom always says "Everything in moderation," but Laura sometimes tends toward "If you're going to do it, do it all out."*

Danielle was set to visit Laura there for three days, and Laura suggested in her email that upon arriving they "convalesce" at an "adorable little café" on Île Saint-Louis, where Danielle was staying. Laura—always the Method actress—signed the email with a cool *Bisous*. Would Brigitte Bardot have written "Xoxo"? Laura thought not.

When we met up, Laura was sporting a pair of black lace-up boots she'd gotten from a vintage store, which she paired with culottes and a white tee. There was also the newsboy cap she was having a kind of on-again, off-again relationship with. To Danielle's dismay, this week the two of them were quite on.

After twenty-five minutes of sitting at the café with no one coming to take their order, Danielle motioned for the server to come over.

"Danielle, no, the waiter will get here when he gets here," Laura said with an Americans-don't-know-how-to-live eye-roll.

"I'm starving! I didn't eat on the plane!" Danielle said. Laura sighed, as if not eating on a plane was *such* an American thing to do as well.

An hour later, after being served croissants and café au laits, we walked over to the Marais to do some shopping. On Laura's favorite street, Rue Charlot, she pointed out Café Charlot, where she'd sat on her own with a croque-monsieur (her regular order) and a carafe of red wine the previous week. Laura had already pointed out about fourteen cafés that were her favorite—all of which she described as either "cute" or "so French"—but this particular one was even more special, as it's where she'd spotted Julia Roberts.

"No one even flinched, Danielle. No one looked up. They don't care about those things here," Laura said.

"How very French," Danielle replied sarcastically.

"They just . . . they know—"

"They know how to live, I know. You said in your email."

We went into a boutique and after looking around for a bit, Danielle exited. Laura gave the saleswoman an apologetic *"Au revoir! Merci!"* before hurrying out after Danielle, lecturing her on how rude it is to leave a store in Paris without saying good-bye and thanking the saleswoman.

"You do know half of the bottom of your shoe is hanging off, don't you?" Danielle responded, changing the subject.

"What do you mean?" Laura asked.

As happens in vintage fashion, all the walking around had destroyed the sole of Laura's shoe, half of which was now hanging off and flapping around. Laura gave a *c'est la vie* shrug, and as they walked past a group of women, they laughed and said something in French to Laura.

"I always get complimented on my outfits here!" she said proudly.

Had the ladies been commenting on Laura's outfit or the state of her shoe? Danielle knew it was the latter but decided to hold her tongue.

"And I get asked for directions like, all the time. Everyone here is so nice," Laura continued. "I just don't get why everyone says French people are unwelcoming."

By dinnertime, the entire sole of Laura's shoe had come off, and she was basically walking around Paris with one bare foot. In fact, the only part of the bottom of the shoe that was still intact was a steel nail attached to cloth that was now digging into Laura's foot. Between the possible tetanus and the newsboy cap this *was* turning into a scene from *Les Misérables.*

"If you keep walking on those you'll have to go to a doctor tomorrow," Danielle said.

"French people don't run to doctors for every little thing like Americans do," Laura said mid-limp.

Laura's laundry list of culture gaps had become as long as *War and Peace.*

Despite her irritation, Danielle continued to encourage Laura to come back to her hotel to borrow shoes, or to go home for a bit to get her own pair, but Laura wouldn't. Still today, Laura loves taking in a city for hours and hours, not letting Danielle go home and shower before dinner. We are the only two girls who somehow look like vagabonds while carrying Céline purses. (It's not a good look during Paris Fashion Week.)

That night we people-watched over a cheese plate and bottle of wine at La Palette on Rue de Seine, then we moved on to foie gras, followed by a heaping plate of *côtes de boeuf* and frites, at Le Vin de Bellechasse. Eating and drinking our way through Paris became the very best part of Danielle's visit, and after a few more bites, all our temporary "cultural differences" were forgotten. It just goes to show that great food always has the power to bring people together—even a dedicated Francophile and an American Tourist.

LAURA'S LAUNDRY LIST OF CULTURE GAPS HAD BECOME AS LONG AS WAR AND PEACE.

Why have a croque-monsieur when you can have a Croque Ma-Soeur? From our take on a grilled cheese to a healthier collard greens wrap, try packing your lunchbox with one of our favorite sandwiches.

CROQUE MA-SOEUR

Makes 4 sandwiches

For the Russian dressing

½ cup mayonnaise

3 tablespoons ketchup

2 tablespoons pickle relish

2 tablespoons grated white onion

1 tablespoon Dijon mustard

1 teaspoon apple cider vinegar

1 teaspoon Worcestershire sauce

Kosher salt and freshly ground pepper

Hot sauce

For the sandwiches

2 tablespoons unsalted butter,
at room temperature

8 thin slices white sandwich bread

¾ pound Gruyère cheese, coarsely grated

1½ cups sauerkraut, well drained

4 thin slices ham

Cornichon pickles, for serving

This is a classic take (okay, more like a non-kosher Jewish sisters' take) on the French classic.

1. Preheat the oven to 400°F. Line a baking sheet with parchment paper.

2. MAKE THE RUSSIAN DRESSING: In a large bowl, mix together the mayo, ketchup, relish, onion, mustard, vinegar, Worcestershire sauce, and salt, pepper, and hot sauce to taste.

3. MAKE THE SANDWICHES: Butter one side of each of the slices of bread and arrange 4 of them buttered side down on the prepared baking sheet.

4. Stir the Gruyère into the Russian dressing. Spread about one-third of the dressing/cheese mixture on the bread slices on the baking sheet. Squeeze as much liquid as possible out of the sauerkraut and divide it among the sandwiches. Top the sauerkraut with a slice of ham, folding it as necessary so it's within the borders of the bread. Spread another one-third of the dressing/cheese mixture on top of the ham. Close the sandwiches with the remaining bread slices, buttered side up, and slather the remaining dressing/cheese mixture on top, being sure to spread it to the edges of the bread.

5. Bake the sandwiches until the top edges are browned, 15 to 17 minutes. Transfer to plates and serve with cornichons alongside.

GREEN GODDESS CHICKEN CLUBS

Makes 4 sandwiches

2 large cooked chicken breast halves, pulled or chopped into bite-size pieces

⅓ cup Green Goddess Dressing (recipe follows), plus more for spreading

Kosher salt and freshly ground pepper

8 slices white sandwich bread, lightly toasted

6 slices bacon, cooked and halved crosswise

2 medium tomatoes, sliced

4 romaine heart leaves

After many, many room-service club sandwiches at hotels (the best), we finally mastered our own. The Green Goddess dressing is key here—and the recipe makes a bit more dressing than you'll need, so save whatever you have left over and use it on a salad later. For the chicken breasts, use store-bought rotisserie chicken or poach chicken breast halves in salted simmering water until cooked through.

1. In a large bowl, combine the chicken and Green Goddess dressing and season with salt and pepper.

2. Arrange 4 slices of toast on a work surface and divide the chicken salad evenly among them. Top each with 3 pieces of bacon, followed by the tomato slices and the romaine. Spread the remaining toast with some more of the dressing. Close up the sandwiches and halve or quarter them, using toothpicks to hold them together.

Green Goddess Dressing
Makes 1 heaping cup

½ cup mayonnaise

½ cup Greek yogurt, preferably 2% or whole-milk

2 tablespoons fresh lemon juice

¼ cup basil leaves

1 tablespoon tarragon leaves

1 tablespoon chopped chives

1 teaspoon anchovy paste

Kosher salt and freshly ground pepper

In a blender or food processor, combine the mayo, yogurt, lemon juice, herbs, and anchovy paste and puree until a pale green sauce forms. Season with salt and pepper.

COLLARD WRAPS WITH FALAFEL, TAHINI SAUCE, AND PICKLES

Makes 4 wraps

¼ cup tahini

2 tablespoons fresh lemon juice

1 small garlic clove, minced

Kosher salt and freshly ground pepper

4 large collard leaves

1 kosher dill pickle, thinly
sliced lengthwise

Easy Baked Falafel (recipe follows)

Wraps can feel a little old-fashioned, but not this one. It's worth cooking up some falafel and having them on hand to make this wrap for an easy lunch—you can even freeze them. This recipe is healthy and really hits the spot.

1. In a small bowl, whisk together the tahini, lemon juice, 2 tablespoons water, and the garlic. Season with salt and pepper.

2. Using a sharp knife, trim the thick stem and cut out the thick rib from the collard leaves. (It will have a V shape at the bottom.) Drizzle about 1 tablespoon sauce over each collard leaf. Top with the pickle slices followed by 2 falafel patties. Drizzle with a little more sauce. Fold in the sides of the leaves to enclose the patties, then tuck in the top and bottom. Halve the wraps and serve.

Easy Baked Falafel

Makes 8 patties

1 cup dried chickpeas

½ small onion, roughly chopped

1 large garlic clove, roughly chopped

½ cup flat-leaf parsley leaves

¼ cup cilantro leaves

1½ tablespoons extra-virgin olive oil, plus more for brushing

1½ tablespoons fresh lemon juice

1 teaspoon ground coriander

½ teaspoon ground cumin

⅛ teaspoon ground cardamom

1½ teaspoons kosher salt

⅛ teaspoon freshly ground black pepper

Pinch of cayenne pepper (optional)

¼ teaspoon baking soda

1. In a large bowl, cover the chickpeas with water by 1 inch and soak for 12 hours.

2. Preheat the oven to 350°F.

3. Drain the chickpeas and transfer to a food processor. Add the onion, garlic, herbs, oil, lemon juice, spices, salt, black pepper, cayenne (if using), and baking soda and process until the mixture is very finely chopped and holds together when squeezed but is not pureed, 30 seconds to 1 minute.

4. Generously brush a large baking sheet with olive oil. Using your hands, form the chickpea mixture into 8 patties and arrange them on the baking sheet. Brush the top sides of the patties with olive oil and bake until golden on the bottom, 12 to 15 minutes. Flip the patties, brush the tops with olive oil, and bake until the patties are set, about 10 minutes longer.

5. Serve hot, warm, or at room temperature.

GRILLED CHEESE AND TOMATO WITH KALE PESTO

Makes 4 sandwiches

3 tablespoons unsalted butter, at room temperature

8 slices (½ inch thick) country white bread

½ cup Kale Pesto (recipe follows) or other pesto

½ pound Fontina cheese, thinly sliced

1 large tomato, thinly sliced

1 ounce Parmigiano-Reggiano cheese, finely grated (about ½ cup)

When we were kids, our grandmother used to take us to Burger Heaven (a New York City establishment with several outposts) for grilled cheese and tomato sandwiches. To this day, if we're near a Burger Heaven, we'll sit at the counter and have one—with a Diet Coke—and it always, always hits the spot. We've upgraded it here a bit with kale pesto, Fontina, and Parmesan, and it is probably one of the most delicious, comforting, and crowd-pleasing recipes in our collection.

1.   Butter one side of each slice of bread. Place 4 of the slices buttered side down on a work surface and spread with the pesto. Arrange half of the Fontina on top, followed by all of the tomato. Sprinkle with Parmesan and layer with the remaining Fontina. Close the sandwiches with the remaining bread slices buttered side up.

2.   Heat a large skillet over medium-low heat. Add the sandwiches and cook until the bottoms of the sandwiches are browned, 4 to 5 minutes. Carefully flip the sandwiches and cook, pressing with a spatula, until the bottoms of the sandwiches are browned and the cheese is melted, about 4 minutes longer.

3.   Transfer the sandwiches to a work surface and let cool slightly. Halve the sandwiches and serve hot.

Kale Pesto

Makes about 1½ cups

Kosher salt

1 bunch kale (about 8 ounces), stemmed

2 medium garlic cloves

½ cup toasted pumpkin seeds

½ cup grated Parmigiano-Reggiano cheese

1 tablespoon fresh lemon juice

¾ cup extra-virgin olive oil

1. Bring a medium pot of salted water to a boil over high heat. Add the kale and garlic and blanch for 1 minute. Immediately drain and run under cold water to stop cooking. Use your hands to squeeze the kale dry.

2. Transfer the kale, garlic, pumpkin seeds, and Parmesan to a food processor and pulse until finely chopped, about 25 pulses. With the motor running, gradually add the lemon juice and olive oil and season with salt.

3. Store the pesto in an airtight container in the refrigerator for up to 3 days or in the freezer for up to 1 month.

TO EAT OR NOT TO EAT
AT FASHION WEEK

Since The New Potato presents the world through the lens of food, we could think of no better angle in covering our first New York Fashion Week than going backstage at runway shows and reporting on what everyone was eating and drinking. The models, the hairstylists, the makeup artists ... what were they consuming while prepping? We were desperate to find out.

Only a year into launching the website, the prospect of it all was so exciting. The fact that we got press passes to a show like Proenza Schouler made us think: *We're really onto something with this approach to food.* Let's skim over the fact we were only invited backstage—not to the show—a topic we conveniently skipped over when other editors would say "See you out there!" and we'd reply with a nonchalant "Totes, see you out there." We hoped everyone just thought we had super-hidden seats that were so exclusive you could never find us.

"We'll do lunch afterward?" Danielle asked Laura as we made our way through security to the backstage entrance.

"We probably won't even need to—I'm sure there will be a great spread. We should taste everything we write about!"

We nodded in agreement and practically considered ourselves the Annie Leibovitz and Frank Rich of the food world.

Our first moments backstage were exciting. We weaved in, out, and around the makeup artists and hairstylists hunched over the models, and found ourselves next to cameras shooting videos for publications like the *New York Times* Style Section. What company for The New Potato to be in! We began to scavenge the scene for gourmet options only the fashion set could get their hands on: Danielle had her camera at the ready for snapping shots, Laura her iPhone in hand for note taking.

The first sign of trouble was a particularly lackluster plate of half-eaten green grapes sitting in front of a model whose hair was being carefully disheveled. Danielle raised her eyebrows: *Grapes? It's lunchtime.*

Laura offered an encouraging nod: *She's a model, she's going light for the show. There's a big spread around here somewhere.*

Danielle shook her head: *I'm not seeing anything.* These were facial-expression conversations only sisters can have.

A makeup artist passed with a black paper plate, featuring more of the aforementioned grapes and a small, lonely-looking block of cheddar cheese. Oh boy. Danielle jutted her head out: *SEE!*

"Sir?" Laura stopped a male hairstylist rushing past them. "Where's the food table?"

"The food table? There's no lunch here."

"Right, but, like, the pass-arounds."

"Um, pass-arounds?"

"Sorry, hors d'oeuvres," Laura corrected, quickly.

The discrepancy between pass-arounds and hors d'oeuvres was not the cause of his confusion.

"There's coconut water over there and if there are snacks or whatever they're not really for press." He shuffled hurriedly away.

Laura looked at Danielle; her imagined exposé on a Michelin chef's finest crab cakes and mini champagne bottles models drank through straws were slipping further and further away. Danielle cocked her head at the ice bucket of boxed coconut water.

Laura spotted an abandoned plate with more types of fruit on it than just grapes—it was practically a fruit salad. She pondered how to make chopped cantaloupe sound more climactic than it is. She was sure Maureen Dowd could do it, so why couldn't she? She suggested Danielle shoot the plate from a few angles: Maybe up top, from the left and right.

"This is not a Cézanne still life," Danielle responded.

She had a point.

_____

In honor of lunching (or not lunching), here are some of our favorite salad recipes.

GREEK CHICKEN SALAD WITH FETA VINAIGRETTE

Serves 4

For the chicken

1 tablespoon fresh lemon juice

1 large garlic clove, grated or minced

½ teaspoon dried oregano

1 tablespoon extra-virgin olive oil, plus more for the grill

2 boneless, skinless chicken breasts, butterflied, or 4 chicken cutlets

Kosher salt and freshly ground pepper

For the salad

2 romaine hearts, chopped

1 pint cherry tomatoes, halved

½ pound cucumber, diced

20 pitted kalamata olives

½ cup chopped flat-leaf parsley

For the dressing

⅓ cup crumbled feta cheese

2 tablespoons red wine vinegar

¼ cup extra-virgin olive oil

1 teaspoon dried oregano

We're admittedly Greek salad snobs. In trying just about every version in New York City, we've discovered the key: It's all about the feta. When the feta mixes well with the vinaigrette, it forms a sort of coating that gets all over everything else in the best way. To ensure the ideal balance every time, we've created a feta vinaigrette. And, well . . . it's perfect.

1. **PREPARE THE CHICKEN:** In a small bowl, combine the lemon juice, garlic, oregano, and olive oil and stir to combine. Brush the marinade all over the chicken. Season with salt and pepper and let stand for 10 minutes or refrigerate for 30 minutes.

2. Preheat a grill or a grill pan over medium-high heat.

3. Rub the grill grates or pan with olive oil. Add the chicken and cook until grill marks appear on the bottom, about 3 minutes. Flip and cook until just opaque throughout, 2 to 3 minutes longer. Transfer the chicken to a cutting board to rest.

4. **MAKE THE SALAD:** In a large bowl, toss together the romaine, tomatoes, cucumber, olives, and parsley.

5. **MAKE THE DRESSING:** In a small bowl, whisk together the feta, vinegar, olive oil, and oregano.

6. Drizzle half the dressing over the salad and toss to coat. Slice the chicken into strips, then add to the salad and toss again. Serve, passing more dressing at the table.

LEMONY FARRO-RADICCHIO SALAD WITH ALMONDS

Serves 2 to 4

1 cup farro

½ cup raw whole almonds

1 medium head radicchio (about 12 ounces)

¼ cup extra-virgin olive oil, plus more for brushing

Kosher salt

¼ cup fresh lemon juice

¼ cup grated ricotta salata

Freshly ground pepper

1. Preheat the oven or toaster oven to 350°F.

2. In a small saucepan, combine the farro with 3 cups water and bring to a boil over high heat. Reduce the heat to medium-low and simmer until the farro is tender, 20 to 25 minutes. Drain and shake out any excess water.

3. Spread the almonds out on a baking sheet and toast until fragrant, about 5 minutes. Let cool, then coarsely chop.

4. Quarter the radicchio lengthwise into wedges. Brush with olive oil and season with salt.

5. Preheat a grill or grill pan over high heat. Add the wedges with one of the cut sides down and cook until charred, about 2 minutes. Turn the wedges so the other cut side is down and cook until charred, another 2 minutes. Transfer to a cutting board and slice the radicchio crosswise.

6. In a large bowl, whisk together the lemon juice, olive oil, and ricotta salata. Add the farro, radicchio, and most of the almonds and toss to combine. Season with salt and pepper. Serve, garnished with the remaining almonds.

TOMATO SALAD WITH GRILLED HALLOUMI AND HERBS

Serves 4

1 pound small to medium best summer
tomatoes, sliced into rounds

½ lemon

Flaky salt and freshly ground pepper

Extra-virgin olive oil

½ pound Halloumi cheese, sliced into
4 slabs

5 basil leaves, torn

2 tablespoons finely chopped
flat-leaf parsley

While we love a good caprese, this salad is a nice way to change it up a little. The salty Halloumi pairs perfectly with the tomato and herbs.

1. Preheat a grill or grill pan over medium-high heat.

2. Arrange the tomatoes on a serving platter or four plates. Lightly squeeze the lemon over them and season with flaky salt and pepper.

3. Brush the grill grates with oil, then add the cheese and cook, turning once, until marks appear and the cheese is warmed throughout, about 1 minute per side. Place on top of the tomatoes. Drizzle the salad with olive oil and sprinkle with the basil and parsley. Serve immediately.

CURRIED SQUASH AND QUINOA SALAD WITH LIME

Serves 4

1 (2-pound) acorn squash, halved, seeded, and cut lengthwise into ½-inch-wide wedges

1 tablespoon virgin coconut oil, melted

½ teaspoon mild curry powder

Kosher salt and freshly ground pepper

1 cup quinoa

1 tablespoon minced shallot

2 tablespoons fresh lime juice, or more to taste

¼ cup extra-virgin olive oil

2 cups baby arugula

The coconut oil is key in this salad—it gives the squash the most delicious flavor. If you hate coconut, stop reading. Just kidding—replace it with olive oil. And don't skip the lime! It adds the perfect brightness.

1.   Preheat the oven to 425°F. Line a baking sheet with parchment paper.

2.   In a large bowl, toss the squash with the coconut oil and curry powder until well coated, then season with salt and pepper. Spread on the lined baking sheet and roast, turning once, until browned and tender, about 30 minutes.

3.   Rinse the quinoa well. In a small pot, combine the quinoa with 2 cups water and bring to a boil over high heat. Cover the pot, reduce the heat to medium, and simmer until the grains are tender, about 15 minutes. Remove the pot from the heat and let stand covered for 5 minutes.

4.   In a large bowl, combine the shallot and lime juice and let stand 5 minutes. Whisk in the olive oil. Add the quinoa and half of the arugula and toss. Season with salt and pepper.

5.   Arrange the quinoa salad on plates or a platter. Top with squash wedges and the remaining arugula and serve.

KALE-AVOCADO CAESAR WITH PECORINO CRUMBLES

Serves 4

Neutral oil, for the skillet

1 cup shredded Pecorino Romano cheese
(about 2 ounces)

1 small garlic clove, smashed and peeled

1 tablespoon Dijon mustard

1 teaspoon Worcestershire sauce

1 Hass avocado

Juice of 1 lemon, or more to taste

Juice of 1 lime, or more to taste

¼ cup plus 2 tablespoons extra-virgin
olive oil

Kosher salt and freshly ground pepper

1 pound Tuscan (lacinato) or curly
kale, stemmed

MAKE AHEAD: *You can make this salad and dress it several hours ahead. Store it, covered, in the refrigerator. Add the cheese crisps just before serving.*

We're not going to pretend we invented the Kale Caesar, but we do have a trick. We like to incorporate avocado into our dressing (rather than egg or cream). It adds the same creaminess—especially when paired with the Dijon—but is obviously much healthier. Top it with some grilled chicken—or, if you're as obsessed as we are, more avocado!

1. In a nonstick skillet, heat a very thin layer of neutral oil over medium heat. Working in batches if necessary, arrange tablespoon-size mounds of pecorino about 1 inch apart and cook until the cheese looks firm and the underside is golden, about 3 minutes. Flip and cook until the cheese is firm and crisp, about 1 minute longer. Transfer to a plate and let cool.

2. In a blender or mini food processor, pulse together the garlic, mustard, Worcestershire sauce, avocado, lemon juice, and lime juice. With the machine on, stream in the olive oil. Season with salt and pepper.

3. In a large bowl, combine the kale leaves and a pinch of salt and massage until the kale is tender. Add the dressing and toss to coat. Just before serving, add the cheese crisps, and toss, allowing the cheese to break down into crumbles.

ORZO SALAD WITH GREEN BEANS, FETA, AND WALNUTS

Serves 4

1½ cups walnut halves

3 tablespoons fresh lemon juice, plus more to taste

1 teaspoon ground coriander

½ teaspoon honey

2 scallions, thinly sliced

1 small garlic clove, finely chopped

Kosher salt

¾ pound haricots verts, cut into 1-inch lengths

1½ cups orzo (7 to 8 ounces), preferably whole wheat

1 cup pitted green olives, halved or quartered (about 6 ounces)

½ cup flat-leaf parsley or cilantro leaves, coarsely chopped

¼ cup extra-virgin olive oil

1½ cups crumbled feta cheese

Crushed red pepper

MAKE AHEAD: *This salad can be refrigerated for up to 12 hours.*

1. Preheat the oven to 350°F.

2. Spread the walnuts out on a baking sheet and toast until fragrant, 4 to 5 minutes. Let cool, then coarsely chop.

3. In a large bowl, combine the lemon juice, coriander, honey, scallions, and garlic.

4. In a large saucepan, bring ½ inch water to a boil over high heat and season with salt. Add the haricots verts, cover, and steam until tender, 2 to 3 minutes. Drain and rinse under cold water. Pat dry and transfer to the bowl with the dressing.

5. Fill the same saucepan with water and bring to a boil over high heat. Season with salt and cook the orzo according to the package directions, until al dente. Drain, then shake dry, and add to the bowl.

6. Add the olives, parsley, olive oil, and 1 cup of the feta to the bowl and toss to combine. Fold in the walnuts. Season with crushed red pepper and more salt and lemon juice, if needed. Sprinkle with the remaining feta and serve.

LEMON-TAHINI SALAD WITH LENTILS, BEETS, AND CARROTS

Serves 2 to 4

3 small beets, scrubbed

¾ cup small green lentils, such as Le Puy

Kosher salt

2 tablespoons fresh lemon juice

3 tablespoons tahini

1 teaspoon honey

Freshly ground pepper

½ cup finely chopped red onion
(from 1 small onion)

1½ cups diced carrots

2 lightly packed cups baby kale

1 romaine heart, chopped

To help this salad come together quickly, you can seek out precooked lentils and vacuum-packed cooked beets at the grocery store.

1. Fill a deep skillet with ½ inch water and bring to a simmer over medium heat. Add the unpeeled beets, cover, and cook until tender, about 20 minutes. Drain and run the beets under cold water to cool. Rub off the skins and dice.

2. Meanwhile, in a small saucepan, combine the lentils and water to cover by 2 inches and bring to a boil over high heat. Cover partially, reduce the heat to medium, and simmer until the lentils are tender, 20 to 25 minutes. Season with salt and let stand 5 minutes, then drain off any excess water.

3. In a large bowl, whisk together the lemon juice, 2 tablespoons water, the tahini, and the honey. Season with salt and pepper. Add the onion and let stand 5 minutes.

4. Add the lentils, carrots, beets, kale, and romaine and toss to combine. Season with salt and pepper. Serve.

ITALIAN TUNA SALAD

Serves 2 to 4

1 medium head butter lettuce, leaves torn into bite-size pieces

1 cup cherry tomatoes, halved

10 small balls fresh mozzarella, halved

½ cup frozen corn kernels, thawed

1 (7-ounce) jar olive-oil-packed tuna, drained

1 tablespoon red wine vinegar

2 tablespoons extra-virgin olive oil

Kosher salt and freshly ground pepper

When Danielle was studying abroad in Milan, she ate a variation of this salad every day for lunch. It seemed impossible to find a version as good in the United States—maybe because of the freshness of the tuna, or the fact that the mozzarella in Italy is the best on earth. But we did our best. (And the result is damn good.)

In a large bowl, toss together the lettuce, tomatoes, mozzarella, corn, and tuna. Add the vinegar and oil and toss gently. Season with salt and pepper and serve.

THE RED LION INN STORY

*T*he Red Lion Inn is an oasis near our grandparents' house in the Berkshires that we'd been going to for dinners and special occasions since childhood. It was also the place where our fates were forever sealed: Danielle established herself as the older, wiser, and virtuous child and Laura became the younger, spoiled, and mischievous child. We know . . . this is starting to sound a little like Fiddler on the Roof.

You see, apparently when Danielle was five years old and Laura was two years old, our grandparents were looking after us while our parents were away. We went to a wonderful dinner at the Red Lion Inn, but for some reason, Laura was being beyond impossible. Sure, she was just a toddler, but as a bystander, you might think she was with evil kidnappers and being absolutely tortured, not with her grandparents at a dinner that was meant to be a nice treat. She screamed and cried, she smacked her plate—she just wasn't happy about anything.

Danielle, on the other hand, not only acted calm, collected, and even-tempered, but after looking Laura up and down, unimpressed by the level of her tantrum, apparently told our grandma something along the lines of "If you just ignore her for a short time, she'll come around. Pretend she's not even here . . . just for a little while."

Now, we know what you're thinking. It's the same thing Laura's been thinking since our Austrian grandma started telling this story twenty years ago: *A five-year-old said that?*

Well, apparently she did, and we imagine she did so right before sending her grape juice back on account of its being "a tad too tart."

Well, the plan worked. They played hard to get with Laura, Laura came around, and Danielle proceeded to triumphantly order her favorite French onion soup.

For our grandma, this story is like a Chanel suit: timeless.

Fast-forward twenty-two years. When Danielle's wedding was about a week away, the whole family had gathered for dinner at the Bowery Hotel. The reception would be there; we were feeling festive and wanted everyone to experience it beforehand. As we sipped our wine, ready to toast the soon-to-be newlyweds, Grandma turned to Laura and said, "Laurtshki, I was thinking I'd tell the Red Lion Inn story at the ceremony."

"Mom?" Laura inquired across the table.

Forget the fact that our grandma was not penciled in for a speech—but all Laura could think was *This madness must be stopped.* And if anyone was going to get roasted at the wedding, the bride was a much better option!

In the end, our grandma never did get to tell the Red Lion Inn story at Danielle's wedding, but you can bet whether it was a graduation, a funeral, or a future wedding, she'd always try to. And speaking of future weddings, if Laura never got married, according to Grandma, the reason could *absolutely* be traced back to her behavior on that fateful night at the Red Lion Inn.

Danielle's favorite dish at the Red Lion Inn was French onion soup—there is nothing like a bowl of the hot stuff to brighten up a cold winter day. Soup's on!

SIMPLEST ONION SOUP WITH POACHED EGGS

Serves 4

3 tablespoons extra-virgin olive oil

1 large onion, halved and thinly sliced

Kosher salt

¼ cup dry white wine

6 cups low-sodium chicken or vegetable broth

Freshly ground pepper

4 large eggs

While we are suckers for a cheesy French onion soup, the egg is a nice change here. Obviously, the runny yolk is awesome, and it sort of feels like breakfast for dinner. Get some crusty bread and dip it in there.

1. In a large pot, heat the olive oil over medium-high heat until warmed. Add the onion and a pinch of salt and cook, stirring, until softened and starting to brown, about 6 minutes. When the onion creates lots of browned bits in the bottom of the pan, add 1 or 2 tablespoons water and scrape to loosen them up. Continue cooking the onion and adding water and scraping as necessary, until the onion slices are a consistent brown color, about 10 minutes longer. Add the wine and cook until evaporated, about 3 minutes. Add the broth and bring to a boil, then reduce the heat to low and simmer for 5 minutes to allow the flavors to meld. Season with salt and pepper.

2. Crack each of 2 eggs into a small bowl or ramekin and slip them into the soup. Cook until the whites are set and the yolks are still runny, 1½ to 2 minutes. Using a slotted spoon, transfer the eggs to soup bowls. Repeat with the remaining 2 eggs. Ladle the soup over the eggs and serve.

CARROT-GINGER SOUP WITH CASHEW BUTTER

Serves 4 to 6

2 tablespoons virgin coconut oil or neutral oil

1 onion, halved and thinly sliced

Kosher salt

1 pound carrots, roughly chopped

1 tablespoon grated fresh ginger (from about 1½ inches)

¼ teaspoon ground turmeric

4 cups unsalted or low-sodium chicken or vegetable broth

¼ cup cashew butter

Freshly ground pepper

Crème fraîche, for garnish (optional)

Roasted pumpkin seeds, for garnish (optional)

Fresh parsley, for garnish

MAKE AHEAD: *This soup can be refrigerated for up to 5 days or frozen for up to 3 months.*

Carrot-ginger soup is what we like to call "a Monica dish." Monica is our mom, and this is one of her go-tos for a dinner party. We upped the ante with a bit of cashew butter and some turmeric, which is not only great for you but also gives the soup a real kick.

1. In a large pot, melt the coconut oil over medium heat. Add the onion, season with salt, and cook, stirring, until softened, about 6 minutes. Add the carrots and ginger and cook, stirring, until fragrant, about 1 minute. Add the turmeric and stir to coat the carrots. Add the broth, increase the heat to high, and bring to a boil. Reduce the heat to medium and simmer until the carrots are soft, 15 to 20 minutes.

2. Use an immersion blender to puree the soup. (Alternatively, ladle the soup into a blender or food processor and let it cool slightly before pureeing.) Add the cashew butter and pulse a few times until incorporated. Season the soup with pepper and more salt. Ladle the soup into bowls, garnish with the crème fraîche and pumpkin seeds, if using. Sprinkle with parsley and a little more pepper, and serve.

OUR CHICKEN SOUP

Serves 4 to 6

1½ pounds boneless, skinless
chicken thighs

1 onion, halved and peeled

6 cups low-sodium chicken broth

½ pound carrots (about 6 small),
cut into ½-inch coins

½ pound parsnips (about 1 large),
cut into ½-inch coins

½ pound red or other waxy potatoes,
peeled and cut into bite-size pieces

2 medium celery ribs, cut into
½-inch slices

Kosher salt and freshly ground pepper

Chopped flat-leaf parsley or dill
(or both!), for garnish

MAKE AHEAD: *This soup can be refrigerated
for up to 3 days or frozen for up to 3 months.*

Nothing will serve you better in life (okay, maybe a few other things) than a perfect, easy, quick, and delicious classic chicken soup recipe. You can simultaneously cure a cold, impress your boyfriend, have a satisfying healthy dinner, and store about a week's worth of leftovers.

1. In a large pot, combine the chicken, onion, and broth and bring to a boil over high heat. Reduce the heat to medium-low and simmer until the chicken is cooked through, about 10 minutes. Using tongs or a slotted spoon, transfer the chicken to a work surface and discard the onion. When the chicken is cool enough to handle, cut it into bite-size pieces.

2. Meanwhile, skim any impurities off the broth (or strain into a clean saucepan). Add the carrots, parsnips, potatoes, and celery and cook over medium heat until all the vegetables are tender, about 15 minutes. Return the chicken to the broth and season with salt and pepper. Ladle the soup into bowls, garnish with parsley, and serve.

SMOKY LENTIL SOUP with GREENS

Serves 4 to 6

1 cup black lentils or small green lentils
(such as Le Puy)

¼ cup extra-virgin olive oil, plus more
for drizzling

1 small onion, finely chopped

1 medium carrot, cut into bite-size pieces

Kosher salt and freshly ground pepper

4 garlic cloves, finely chopped

2 tablespoons tomato paste

1 teaspoon chopped fresh rosemary or
½ teaspoon dried

8 cups low-sodium chicken or vegetable
broth or water

½ teaspoon smoked paprika

1 bunch (about 8 ounces) kale, Swiss
chard, or young collards, tough stems
and central ribs removed, leaves
finely chopped

1 tablespoon sherry vinegar

NOTE: *Try topping this soup with cheese toasts. In a 350°F oven, toast 4 to 6 thick slices of baguette for about 10 minutes. Ladle the soup into bowls and top with the toasts. Dividing evenly, sprinkle 1 cup grated Gruyère cheese over the bowls. Pop the soups under the broiler for about 2 minutes, until the cheese is melted and bubbling, then serve.*

1. In a bowl, combine the lentils and water to cover by 1 inch. Let soak while you prepare the broth.

2. In a large pot, heat the olive oil over medium heat until warmed. Add the onion and carrot, season with salt and pepper, and cook until softened, about 8 minutes. Add the garlic and cook until softened, 1 to 2 minutes. Add the tomato paste and rosemary and cook until the tomato paste glazes the bottom of the pot, 1 to 2 minutes.

3. Add the broth and smoked paprika to the pot. Drain the lentils and add to the pot. Bring the broth to a boil, then reduce the heat to medium-low and simmer, uncovered, until the lentils are nearly tender, about 30 minutes.

4. Add the chopped greens and cook until tender, about 5 minutes. Add the vinegar and cook for about 30 seconds. Season the soup with salt and pepper. Divide the soup among bowls, drizzle with olive oil, and serve.

EASY PHO

Serves 4 to 6

For the broth

1 large onion, quartered (skin on)

1 (3-inch) piece fresh ginger,
halved lengthwise

1½ pounds beef shin or beef chuck

2 pounds marrow bones

10 black peppercorns

4 whole cloves

1 star anise

1 cinnamon stick

For the soup

½ pound sirloin steak

8 ounces rice stick noodles

2 tablespoons fish sauce, plus more
to taste

1 tablespoon light brown sugar,
plus more to taste

Kosher salt

1 cup mung bean sprouts
(about 2 ounces)

Cilantro leaves and sliced scallion,
for garnish

Lime wedges, Sriracha sauce, and hoisin
sauce (optional), for serving

MAKE AHEAD: *The broth can be refrigerated for up to 3 days or frozen for up to 2 months.*

Pho is one of our favorite meals on the planet. Being able to make our own is a game changer. Thanks to the popularity of bone broth and the Paleo diet, marrow bones are easier than ever to find (try your local Whole Foods or specialty market), so we promise you won't have an issue there—they're key to making a deeply flavorful broth. You'll simmer this soup for 3 to 4 hours—and it's worth it for the flavor. When serving, we like to use lean sirloin, which cooks in seconds when you ladle the hot broth over it.

1. **MAKE THE BROTH:** Preheat the broiler. Arrange the onion and ginger on a baking sheet and broil, turning once, until well charred, about 8 minutes per side.

2. Meanwhile, in a large pot, cover the meat and bones with water and bring to a boil over high heat. Reduce the heat to medium and simmer for about 15 minutes, until the water looks very murky. Drain the bones and rinse well.

3. Rinse the pot, then return the meat and bones to it. Cover with 10 cups fresh water and bring to a boil over high heat. Reduce the heat to maintain a simmer. Add the charred ginger and onion, the peppercorns, cloves, star anise, and cinnamon and simmer very gently until the broth is very flavorful, 3 to 4 hours.

4. Strain the broth into a large bowl (discard the meat and bones). Skim off any fat that rises to the surface, or, if time allows, refrigerate the broth for several hours until the fat solidifies and then skim.

5. **MAKE THE SOUP:** About 20 minutes before you want to prepare the soup, place the steak in the freezer to firm up (this will make it easier to slice).

6. Bring a large pot of water to a boil over medium-high heat. Add the noodles and cook until just barely tender. Drain and rinse under cold water. Divide among soup bowls.

7. Using a sharp knife, slice the steak as thinly as possible and add it to the bowls.

8. If the broth is not already hot, bring it to a boil in a large saucepan. Add the fish sauce and brown sugar, then season to taste with salt. Add more fish sauce and brown sugar, if desired. Ladle the hot broth into the bowls. Use chopsticks to swirl the soup and cook the beef.

9. Top the soup with the bean sprouts. Garnish with cilantro and scallion. If desired, serve with lime wedges, Sriracha, and hoisin sauce to pass at the table.

KATIE COURIC DRIVES AN UBER

*C*ameos are by far the most enjoyable and most nerve-racking part of the videos we produce on *The New Potato*. We get talent for ten minutes at a time, and more often than not, the oh-so-organized script we've put together has not, and will not, be looked at. And why should it? When you're asking Katie Couric (a woman who had to move her meeting time twice because she was interviewing Gloria Steinem and then the president of Planned Parenthood) to appear in a video playing an Uber driver, you should be grateful she even shows up.

But let's back up: We had interviewed Katie Couric over tea at Sarabeth's on the Upper East Side a week before we were to shoot our video spoofing Uber. We had secured video guest cameos, like blogger Bryanboy and Linda Rodin, but felt we needed one more big name to really get it out there.

On our way to the interview, we mused on possibly asking Katie. Serendipitously, we completely hit it off with her. Two hours of shooting, interviewing, and chatting seemed to speed by in five minutes. By the end of the tea, Katie said something like "I love what you girls are doing. If there's anything I can do for you, don't hesitate to let me know."

Laura's eyes widened: *Like play an Uber driver?* We were having one of our telepathic conversations.

Danielle squinted: *I'm just not sure we can ask that now. . . .*

Laura's head slightly tilted: *Come on . . . why not?*

Danielle shrugged: *I mean if you really think it's appropriate, go for it.*

Laura's eyebrows raised: *Right, of course it has to be me. As usual.*

Danielle's head moved forward: *What's that supposed to mean?*

Laura leaned back: *You know exactly what it means.*

Danielle squinted again: *Have it your way, then.*

"Actually," Danielle said, with all the aggressiveness she could muster (i.e., not a lot), "we're shooting this spoof video about Uber. . . ."

The rest, as they say, is history. Katie was scheduled to appear in the video the very next week. We were to meet her in the lobby of Yahoo, go downtown, and shoot the scene in a car we'd park right outside her next appointment. She only had five to ten minutes to shoot, but we'd have time to go over things in the car ride, so we felt okay about it. Plus, we were shooting on Laura's birthday, which we considered a good omen.

While Laura had spent the week obsessing over the script, shots, locations, timing, and where the guys would park for Katie, Danielle had spent the time working on quite a different task: homemade peanut butter.

Katie had told us in her interview that her new obsession was grind-your-own honey peanut butter from Whole Foods, so we thought

it would be a cute idea to bring her a jar or two as a thank-you. While most people would average around twenty-seven minutes on a task such as this, including travel time, Danielle averaged around five and a half business days.

You see, despite her typically laid-back personality, Danielle was that kid in school with perfect penmanship, whose arts and crafts projects were always frustratingly perfect, who would throw out a brand-new journal if a doodle on just one of its pages wasn't up to snuff. Artistic? OCD? Potato, potahto.

Since Katie's preferred peanut butter wasn't jarred, but rather a serve-yourself situation, Danielle took to the kitchen. She spent hours soaking two preexisting jars so she could scrape their labels off entirely and make her own labels, then picked out the most fanciful ribbon to finish them. Whether or not the video went up in smoke, it was safe to say we were set on the peanut-butter front.

Our video guys were ready to go at the parking spot an hour before we showed up, and we waited in the lobby of Yahoo—printed scripts in hand (in case Katie hadn't read the digital version yet)—all set to go downtown.

The moment Katie entered the lobby we knew something was wrong. She talked hurriedly on her phone, and her assistant asked us to get in the car so we weren't "forgotten" when she got in.

Laura clutched the scripts in her hand nervously, reading through Katie's lines. Danielle clutched the peanut butter.

When Katie got in the car, her assistant explained to us she was having a bit of a media crisis concerning a tweet. As we got closer and closer to downtown, Laura took to her phone, to a group text with Danielle and our dad. The thread looked something like this:

● ● ●

LAURA: Dad, help! Katie's having some sort of media situation, no time to look over the script; not sure how to pull it off.

WHETHER OR NOT THE VIDEO WENT UP IN SMOKE, IT WAS SAFE TO SAY WE WERE SET ON THE PEANUT- BUTTER FRONT.

DAD: What about going over lines when you get there?

LAURA: We have five minutes once we get there, and that's to shoot!

DAD: Did you give her the peanut butter??

LAURA: That's really not the priority right now.

DANIELLE: I will once she's off the phone.

LAURA: Guys, forget the peanut butter.

DAD: Does she know it's your birthday?

This was going no place.

Laura and Danielle eyed each other nervously. It sounded like Katie was wrapping up her call.

Danielle's eyes widened: *Finally.* Looks to peanut butter. *She'll love it.*

Laura shook her head: *Script first, then peanut butter.*

Danielle skeptically shrugged: *If you really think so.*

Laura's eyes narrowed: *I really really think so.*

When Katie got off the phone, we were a block away from our destination. She was still voicing concerns to her assistant, but once realizing how close we were she turned to us and said something like "Okay, so sorry, girls, so I have five minutes—what are we doing?"

"Well, so you're going to be the Uber driver—" Laura nervously pulled out the script.

"No, no," Katie said. "Just tell me what I'm saying."

When someone says "Just tell me what I'm saying" and what he or she is saying is ten different lines of back-and-forth dialogue, there's no good way to answer that.

"Here!" Danielle practically shouted, handing over the bag of peanut butter jars.

"Thank you," Katie said, putting it next to her. "So I'm the Uber driver and I just act like I'm doing it for extra pocket money, I tell Laura she has a bad rating, et cetera?"

"Exactly," Laura said. Katie urgently turned back to her assistant in the front. Danielle looked ruefully at the peanut butter.

Danielle glanced at Laura: *Perhaps I pulled the trigger too early.*

Laura took a deep breath: *Stop.*

As soon as the car stopped, we were out in a flash. Laura was yelling, "This way, Katie, they're right here. Sorry, this way!" We were running frantically on either side of her, feeling the need to surround her with our arms as if we were playing London Bridge Is Falling Down. We were doing everything short of carrying Katie Couric.

The sound guy came up, about to say something about Katie's microphone, but before he could even speak she whisked it out of his hand and had mic'd herself up by the time she got to the driver's seat.

We don't really know what happened next, because we're pretty sure we blacked out. But we got a hysterical cameo part with Katie Couric as an Uber driver, and we somehow did it in four minutes.

As for the peanut butter, well, much to Danielle's dismay, we never found out what happened to it.

Peanut butter or something else, there's nothing like a sweet, healthy snack to pick you up around eleven a.m., four p.m., or whenever else you need it.

HONEY PEANUT BUTTER GRANOLA

Makes about 6 cups

½ cup natural peanut butter

⅓ cup honey

1 teaspoon kosher salt

1 teaspoon ground cinnamon

2 cups rolled oats

1 cup buckwheat groats

1 cup quinoa

1 cup coconut flakes

1 cup dried cherries

MAKE AHEAD: *The granola can be kept in an airtight container for up to 2 weeks.*

1. Preheat the oven to 275°F. Line a baking sheet with parchment paper.

2. In a large bowl, whisk together the peanut butter, honey, salt, and cinnamon. Add the oats, buckwheat, and quinoa and stir to coat. Spread the mixture out evenly on the prepared baking sheet and bake for 30 minutes, stirring every 10 minutes.

3. Scatter the coconut over the granola and stir to incorporate, then return to the oven and bake until the granola is golden and fragrant, about 10 minutes longer. (It will not seem fully crisp, but don't worry—it will crisp as it cools.)

4. Transfer the baking sheet to a wire rack to cool. Add the cherries to the granola and toss.

EVENING

TACOS AND TEQUILA
WITH GEORGE AND AMAL

*I*n December 2014, our family went to Cabo with a few other families. Seth, Danielle's husband, joined us, as he always did on our holiday vacations. To get an idea of the kind of value Seth adds to trips, or really to any situation, think Chris Pratt meets Ty Burrell. With Seth, we always have more fun.

One night everyone was at dinner at the One & Only resort, crooning over shrimp and mahi-mahi tacos, when the offer to go to a soirée at George Clooney's house came about. Standard stuff. Our family friends knew the crowd that rolled with George, and when they made the casual suggestion to stop by his house after dinner, the three of us accepted with an attempt at the sort of it's-to-be-expected casualness a person might project when asked if they'd like to look at the dessert menu.

To us (and we're pretty sure to everyone), this wasn't *a* celebrity having a party, this was *the* celebrity having a party. This moment affirmed our steadfast belief that there are, in fact, only a few degrees of separation between us and George Clooney.

On the ride over, we attempted to temper our excitement, especially since everyone else was acting like a grown-up. Laura and Seth in particular were at that point during an evening of drinking where you should have gone home fifty-five minutes prior.

The food in Mexico had been wreaking havoc on Danielle's stomach, so she was avoiding alcohol and was by far the most sensible. We decided that if anyone was going to make small talk with George for any reason, it should be Danielle. This was a responsible, well-thought-out joint decision that Seth forgot about the moment we stepped out of the car.

Golf carts shuttled us from the top of the driveway to George's house. We speculated. *Would George want to take a selfie? Perhaps Hugh Hefner would be there. Who was the surprise musical guest that night?*

We entered a modern, sophisticated lair that was the stuff of James Bond films. The space was very open; you walked in and saw stairs to the upper level whose hallway was exposed. We could only imagine the ins and outs of what went on in that hallway and in those rooms—a collection of tales we like to think of as *The Everyday Adventures of George*.

The lower level was an expansive space that opened up to an infinity pool. Guests were scattered everywhere, as was Casamigos tequila—George's liquor brand.

Danielle admired the architecture as well as the guests, an impressive smattering that included folks like Cindy Crawford, Rande Gerber, and George's now wife, Amal Clooney (then known to us only as the gorgeous woman who somehow snagged George Clooney for

a night). As for George's most esteemed guests—Laura and Seth—well, they were now seventy-two minutes past the time when they should have gone home, and they decided the only thing that made sense was to order drinks.

Now that we were properly equipped with Casamigos cocktails, the mingling could finally begin. Mingling is a broad term, but in this case it was defined by Seth circling Clooney's group like a shark, coming back to us (waiting nervously in the corner) and saying "I'm going to do it, this time I'm doing it!" then leaving before we could attempt to restrain his six-two frame.

We had learned long ago that the only way to deal with a mission of Seth's on a night out was either to let it happen or to redirect his focus. In this case, on Seth's fifth or sixth loop back, redirection came—in the form of Michael Phelps.

The now twenty-three-gold-medal Olympic swimmer was talking to a gorgeous blonde and, according to the bro code, that meant he was not to be bothered. But Seth was not in a state to recognize that, and suddenly his concentrated paces around George became concentrated paces around Michael.

Everyone has a move when it comes to flirting, but Seth's go-to move applies to females, males, celebrities, cultural icons, presidents, and royalty alike. Being tall, he puts his hand on your shoulder and gives you an encouraging little rub. It's a sort of how-you-doing-it's-all-going-to-be-okay movement if you seem off, a welcome-to-the-fold movement if you've just arrived to a party where you don't know anyone, or even a you-can-do-better movement if you've just been broken up with.

This move works on many, but it's safe to say Michael Phelps didn't need to be told any of those things.

It was after two back rubs, both of which Phelps ignored, that we considered intervening. But we were far more comfortable eating soft tacos and being secondhand embarrassed in the corner. The third rub went on for a good seven to ten seconds, then at what seemed like second eleven, Phelps finally, slowly turned.

With that, Seth said, as if he'd just been reunited with an old college buddy, "How's it going, man?"

To quell what's now known to us as the most awkward moment in history, Seth pointed to our corner and said, "My wife's a big fan, she wanted to say hi." Michael was nonplussed, Danielle covered her face, and Laura tipsily giggled.

We wish we could tell you we ran with giants that night. We wish we could tell you we laughed with Cindy, rubbed elbows with Rande, and danced the night away with George and Amal. But at least we had tequila and tacos.

WE HAD LEARNED LONG AGO THAT THE ONLY WAY TO DEAL WITH A MISSION OF SETH'S ON A NIGHT OUT WAS EITHER TO LET IT HAPPEN OR TO REDIRECT HIS FOCUS.

There's nothing like a weekend in Cabo with Clooney to get you in the mood for tacos—and there is nothing we love more than a good taco. Here are our favorite versions!

CHICKEN TINGA TACOS

Makes 8 tacos

For the filling

Extra-virgin olive oil

2 pounds trimmed boneless, skinless chicken thighs

Kosher salt and freshly ground pepper

1 small yellow onion, roughly chopped

4 garlic cloves, roughly chopped

1 teaspoon ancho chile powder

1 teaspoon ground cumin

½ teaspoon ground coriander

½ teaspoon dried oregano, preferably Mexican

¼ teaspoon ground allspice

1 (28-ounce) can tomato puree

For the tacos

8 corn tortillas

Diced white onion, for serving

Cilantro leaves, for serving

Cotija cheese (optional; grated or crumbled), for serving

1. **MAKE THE FILLING:** In a large pot, heat 2 tablespoons olive oil over medium-high heat until shimmering. Season the chicken all over with salt and pepper. Working in batches, add the chicken to the hot oil in a single layer and cook until browned on one side, about 6 minutes. Flip the pieces and cook until browned, about 6 minutes longer. Transfer the chicken to a plate and repeat with the remaining chicken, adding more olive oil as needed.

2. Pour the fat out of the pan and heat 2 more tablespoons olive oil over medium heat until warmed. Add the chopped onion and garlic and cook, stirring occasionally, until softened, about 10 minutes. Add the spices and herbs and cook, stirring, until fragrant, about 30 seconds. Add the tomato puree and bring to a boil over high heat. Reduce the heat to medium and return the chicken to the pot.

3. Simmer, covered, for 10 minutes, then uncover and simmer until the meat pulls easily with a fork and the sauce is thick, about 20 minutes longer. Use two forks to shred the chicken.

4. **PREPARE THE TACOS:** In a dry skillet set over medium heat, toast the tortillas one or two at a time, turning, until fragrant and pliable, 30 seconds to 1 minute each. Wrap in foil or a clean towel to keep warm.

5. Spoon the filling into the tortillas and serve, passing the diced onion, cilantro, and Cotija (if using) at the table.

LAURA: I just can't decide . . . it feels a bit Arya Stark, *Game of Thrones*.

DANIELLE: It's a valid point.

LAURA: Like when she's by the seaside selling shellfish from a basket.

DANIELLE: Ya, the "Oysters, clams, and cockles!!!" part. I totally see it.

LAURA: Well, it's a bad thing to see it.

DANIELLE: Your call. I'm with the bride, can't text back and forth!

While Laura pondered her hairdo, Danielle and the wedding party were getting festive while getting ready. Thanks to the excellent service at Blue Hill, champagne glasses were diligently refilled every six and a half seconds. Danielle joked to the bride, "Laura got this hairdo but she's worried she looks like Arya Stark on *Game of Thrones*," showing her the photo.

"OMG. No, it's so cool she has to keep it!" Lauren said, looking at the photo. "Tell her the bride says keep it!" Danielle texted this to Laura.

• • •

LAURA: I mean, you've sort of backed me into a corner now.

DANIELLE: You can still take it out if you really feel strongly.

LAURA: A Sicilian can never refuse a request on his daughter's wedding day.

DANIELLE: Enough with the *Godfather* references. Please.

So that day, Arya Stark attended her first wedding since the Red Wedding.

The ceremony was beautiful, and afterward the intimate group of sixty was ushered onto the porch to enjoy cocktails and hors d'oeuvres before lunch. There were mushroom sliders, fresh-picked radishes, and ramps and goat cheese on sesame crackers.

Laura glided around the room with a glass of Chardonnay, collecting appetizers and accepting compliments on her hairdo. In the meantime, Danielle tried desperately to make good on her bridesmaid's duties while getting to each appetizer. She'd reach for a slider with one hand, and the hem of the bride's dress with the other.

Danielle eyed the caviar tray close to Laura and gave her a look: *So are you going to help me here?*

Laura raised her eyebrows: *There's only two left, and Grandma Eli is clearly getting to one of them before me.*

Danielle's jaw clenched: *I've barely had any!*

Laura paused: *The braids are a hit, right?!*

Danielle let out a deep breath: *Seriously?*

Laura smiled: *I know, such a great call.*

Laura took the last blini and everyone was ushered into the dining room for lunch.

The meal was a big success, replete with courses like a farm-fresh egg with asparagus, and grass-fed beef with polenta. Danielle, unfortunately, was still hungry. Her husband, Seth, was the best man and had made her leave the reception every five minutes to practice his speech over and over again. At this point, Danielle mouthed it along with him. She knew it like she had known her haftarah portion for her Bat Mitzvah.

"Should it be 'so *let's* raise a glass,'" Seth asked, the two of them standing outside the bathroom, "or 'so let's raise a *glass*'?"

"Wait, what's the difference?" Danielle sighed.

"Do I emphasize *let's* or *glass*?"

"I REALLY DON'T KNOW. BOTH?"

"BOTH? THAT'S INSANE."

THAT'S INSANE? DANIELLE THOUGHT.

Seth asked, as if this was the most obvious question in the world.

"I really don't know. Both?" Danielle said, hoping this was an answer that would get her back to her polenta.

"Both? That's insane."

THAT's insane? Danielle thought.

Danielle finally got back to the table only to learn that her tablemates had made fast work of finishing her food: This was Blue Hill at Stone Barns, after all, and no one was messing around. Seth's speech, on the other hand, went splendidly.

When the reception started to wind down, we took the flip-flops they handed out to guests, and took a walk in the vegetable fields.

"The food here is just insane," Laura said, looking out. "The only thing I didn't get to try was that fresh radish. I am pissed I missed that."

Danielle stopped dead in her tracks and glared at Laura.

"What?" Laura said, turning, touching her hair. "Do I have a flyaway?"

Blue Hill at Stone Barns gave us much inspiration, but you don't have to be head chef Dan Barber to make elegant appetizers that are creative, delicious, and satisfying. . . .

CURRIED SALMON SLIDERS WITH CUCUMBER RAITA

Makes 12 sliders

1½ pounds salmon, skinned and
roughly chopped

2 teaspoons curry powder

1 teaspoon grated lemon zest

Kosher salt and freshly ground pepper

1 cup whole-milk yogurt

2 teaspoons fresh lemon juice

1 scallion, thinly sliced

Small pinch of ground coriander

Small pinch of ground cumin

1 cup diced cucumber

¼ cup finely chopped cilantro

Neutral oil, for the skillet and sliders

12 slider rolls, split and toasted

Butter lettuce leaves, torn

1. In a food processor, combine the salmon with the curry powder, lemon zest, ½ teaspoon salt, and a few grinds of pepper and pulse until finely chopped but not pureed. Form the salmon into 12 small patties, each about ¾ inch thick, and refrigerate until chilled, 15 to 20 minutes.

2. In a medium bowl, mix together the yogurt, lemon juice, scallion, coriander, cumin, cucumber, and cilantro. Season the raita with salt and pepper.

3. Lightly rub a large nonstick skillet with some neutral oil and heat over medium-high heat. Brush the sliders on both sides with oil and lightly season the patties with salt and pepper. Add half of the sliders to the skillet and cook, turning once, until medium, 3 to 4 minutes each. Transfer to a clean plate and repeat with the remaining patties.

4. Arrange the roll bottoms on a serving platter and top with lettuce. Place a patty on top of each leaf and spoon some cucumber raita over each. Close the sliders and serve.

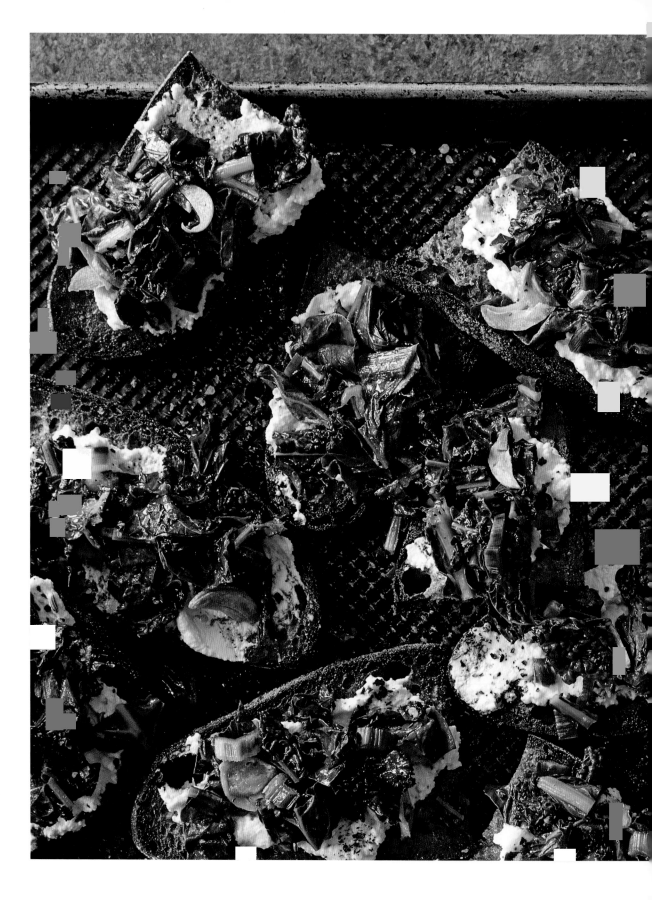

RICOTTA TOASTS WITH GARLICKY GREENS

Makes 8 toasts

For the ricotta

1 cup whole-milk ricotta cheese

1 tablespoon extra-virgin olive oil

½ teaspoon herbes de Provence

Kosher salt and freshly ground
black pepper

For the greens

2 tablespoons extra-virgin olive oil

2 garlic cloves, thinly sliced

8 ounces greens, such as kale,
Swiss chard, or collards, tough stems
and central ribs removed, leaves
finely chopped

Kosher salt and crushed red pepper

4 slices (½ inch thick) bread, cut from
a large peasant-style loaf, toasted

1. **PREPARE THE RICOTTA:** In a small bowl, stir together the ricotta, olive oil, and herbes de Provence. Season with salt and black pepper. Refrigerate until ready to use.

2. **PREPARE THE GREENS:** In a large skillet, heat the olive oil over medium heat until warmed. Add the garlic and cook, stirring, until it starts to turn golden, 1 to 2 minutes. Add the greens and 2 tablespoons water, cover, and cook, stirring occasionally, until the leaves are wilted and tender, about 5 minutes. Season with salt and a pinch of crushed red pepper.

3. Halve the toasts and spread them with ricotta. Spoon the greens on top and serve.

WHEN PALEO MEETS PICASSO

*I*t was on an uneventful Thursday that Laura decided to go Paleo forever. The Paleo diet is *based on foods presumed to have been eaten by early humans, so it mainly consists of meat, fish, vegetables, and fruit. While you might be thinking she was doing this for an article she was writing on The New Potato, that actually had nothing to do with it. Laura had read a Facebook status about a woman who had changed her lifestyle and begun what they call the "caveman diet"—resulting in glowing skin, clarity of thought, and a smorgasbord of other benefits.*

Forty-seven minutes into her new life, Laura exclaimed, "I feel like a different person!"

Danielle tried persuading Laura to get through a week before claiming life-changing effects. "You read this Paleo thing last night, no?" Danielle asked.

"Yes, what's your point?"

"It just may make sense to start with a trial period before committing to a lifelong decision," Danielle said.

Laura chuckled. She didn't need to *try* this out, she was eating only what was directly sourced from the earth from now on. Anything else seemed like blasphemy.

This has been the dynamic since we were kids. Laura lives in a world of black and white, while Danielle sees gray. After Laura saw the movie *Center Stage,* she begged our dad to buy a year's worth of dance lessons.

"Dance is my passion. It's my life now, Dad."

"A yearlong membership?" our mom said. "How about you try one class first?"

Clearly nothing had changed with age, and Laura still has 364 days' worth of dance lessons at her disposal in the suburbs of Connecticut.

Paleo Laura couldn't have arrived on a worse day, as we'd been invited to a party at Leonard Lauder's (Estée Lauder's son) Upper East Side apartment. The soirée was sure to boast more amazing food and drink than anyone could ask for. Laura vowed to have a snack beforehand, and when it came to the question of alcohol, apparently this was the one thing Laura was willing to go gray on.

The party—which took place on a two-story terrace practically dangling over Central Park—included every kind of New York celebrity. Models like Kendall Jenner, powerhouses like Hearst's president, David Carey, and style movers and shakers like the *New York Times*'s chief fashion critic, Vanessa Friedman. No matter who you were, you waited to kiss the ring. Leonard sat perched on a stool as each guest awkwardly came and stood for a shot taken by the Billy Farrell Agency.

We waited awkwardly, and to our disappointment more important guests kept getting ushered in front of us for a photo.

Laura's eyes narrowed: *I told you not to wear a crop top to this.*

Danielle raised her eyebrows: *It's you who's looking at the appetizers like a serial killer.*

A tray whizzed by. Laura looked longingly. "Do you think that's Paleo?"

"Goat cheese and watercress on puff pastry? Something tells me no," Danielle responded.

Once we had our photo taken with Mr. Lauder, the party moved downstairs so guests could view his private collection of Picasso paintings. We were ushered into what looked more like a museum than an apartment.

Before we could even start perusing, though, there it was: the most expansive table of appetizers either of us had ever seen. It was overflowing with olives, cheeses, breads, and cured meats as far as the eye could see. We were completely entranced by the hors d'oeuvres mecca—forget the fact that fifty original Picassos surrounded us.

Before the words could even form on Laura's lips, Danielle responded: "Nope, not Paleo."

While Danielle delved into the aged cheddar, smoked Gouda, Emmental Grand Cru, and soppressata, Laura attempted to busy herself with a forgotten plate of crudités.

But then a waiter came by with a tray of caviar and blini. Laura knew cavemen hadn't had caviar and blini at their disposal. But then again the cavemen had never been offered it at Leonard Lauder's house while standing in front of a collection of Picassos.

And that's how a lifelong Paleo commitment went up in smoke, after seven hours. It just goes to show that truly great appetizers can outshine certain passions, and on very special occasions, can even outshine a certain Picasso.

As long as we're on the topic of appetizers, here are a few more that could keep us distracted from Picassos. Good appetizers never get old, wouldn't you agree?

EGGPLANT-YOGURT DIP

Makes about 2 cups

1 pound eggplant, sliced into rounds

2 tablespoons extra-virgin olive oil, plus more for brushing

Kosher salt and freshly ground pepper

1 large garlic clove, thinly sliced

½ teaspoon cumin seeds

1 (7-ounce) container whole-milk or 2% Greek yogurt

1 tablespoon fresh lemon juice

Chopped flat-leaf parsley or mint (optional), for garnish

Warmed pitas, for serving

For a while, Laura was obsessed with making eggplant dip from a Barefoot Contessa cookbook, but eventually it evolved into making her own version—one we're certain Ina's husband, Jeffrey, would still love. It is super-easy, melts in your mouth, and—especially when served with warm pita—is a tremendous crowd-pleaser. You can also serve it as a spread or alongside a plate of lentils.

1. Heat a grill or preheat a broiler to high. Brush the eggplant rounds on both sides with olive oil and season with salt and pepper. Grill or broil (on a baking sheet) until the eggplant is deeply browned on one side, about 5 minutes. Flip the rounds and grill or broil until the other side is browned and the eggplant is very tender. Let cool slightly, then remove the eggplant peel and transfer the flesh to a large bowl.

2. In a small skillet, heat the olive oil over medium heat. Add the garlic and tip the pan so the garlic cooks in the pooled oil until softened, 1 to 2 minutes. Add the cumin seeds and cook until fragrant, about 20 seconds. Scrape the oil, garlic, and cumin into the bowl with the eggplant.

3. Add the yogurt and lemon juice and stir to combine. Season with salt and pepper. If desired, garnish with parsley or mint. Serve with warmed pitas.

SUPER SAVORY SEED-CRUSTED ASPARAGUS

Serves 4 to 6

Neutral oil, for the pan

½ cup raw pumpkin seeds

¼ cup furikake seasoning (see Note)

1 tablespoon cornstarch

Pinch of cayenne pepper

Kosher salt

1 large egg

1 pound medium-thick asparagus
(about 20 spears), trimmed

NOTE: *Furikake seasoning includes sesame seeds, nori seaweed, bonito (dried fish) flakes, salt, sugar, and sometimes MSG. You can find MSG-free versions at natural food markets, like Whole Foods. After you try this mixture, you'll want to dust it on everything.*

Roasted asparagus has always been a go-to for us, but we always sort of wanted to be able to pick them up with our hands and eat them like French fries (this is frowned upon at dinner; we've tried it). So, we came up with these Asian-inspired asparagus sticks, which will be a massive hit at your next dinner party. You're welcome.

1.   Preheat the oven to 400°F. Line two baking sheets with parchment paper and lightly coat with oil. Preheat the pans for 5 minutes.

2.   In a mini food processor, pulse the pumpkin seeds. (Alternatively, put the seeds in a small resealable bag and use a rolling pin to crush them.) Transfer to a shallow bowl and mix with the furikake, cornstarch, and pinch of cayenne. Taste and season with salt as needed. In a second shallow bowl, beat the egg.

3.   Make sure the asparagus is very dry. Dip the top halves of each spear in the egg and then dredge through the seed mixture. Transfer to a plate.

4.   Arrange the asparagus on the preheated baking sheets and roast for 4 minutes. Flip over each spear and roast until they are just tender, about 4 minutes longer. Transfer to a serving platter and serve.

WINTER SQUASH AND PUMPKIN SEED SPREAD

Makes about 2 cups

1½ pounds acorn squash, halved
lengthwise and seeded

Extra-virgin olive oil

Kosher salt

1 large garlic clove, unpeeled

1 cup pumpkin seeds

¼ cup cilantro sprigs

2 tablespoons fresh lime juice

Freshly ground pepper

Pita chips or crisp vegetables,
for serving

MAKE AHEAD: *The spread can be
refrigerated for up to 2 days.*

1. Preheat the oven to 350°F. Line a baking sheet with parchment paper.

2. Coat the cut sides of the squash with olive oil, season with salt, and set cut sides down on the baking sheet. Rub the garlic with olive oil and set it next to the squash. Bake the squash until very soft, 40 to 45 minutes. Let cool.

3. While the squash bakes, spread the pumpkin seeds out on another baking sheet or a sheet of foil and toast until fragrant, about 5 minutes. Let cool.

4. In a food processor, pulse the pumpkin seeds until finely chopped. Scrape the squash from the skins (you should have about 1½ cups) and add to the processor. Squeeze the garlic from the peel into the processor. Pulse to incorporate. Add the cilantro and lime juice and pulse until combined. Season the spread with salt and pepper and serve with pita chips or crisp vegetables.

A VEGAN LUNCH WITH CHER HOROWITZ

*W*hen we first started the site, we were excited by the prospect of working in Los Angeles. Our West Coast trips would be a respite from our fast-paced New York lifestyle, and driving around and photographing celebrities there for the site would look something like the lead-in to *Entourage*.

Then we met LA traffic. We'd see on Google Maps that a destination was 1.8 miles away and think *Great, we'll leave ourselves seven minutes,* which seemed generous. Fast-forward to twenty-seven minutes later and we'd be sitting behind an Audi TT on Sunset Boulevard, cursing the heavens and apologizing frantically to a publicist over the phone.

Remember that line in *Clueless* where Cher's dad yells over the phone: "Everywhere in LA takes twenty minutes!"? If he meant that even a coffee spot seven hundred feet from your car takes at least twenty minutes or more, then he was correct. Seriously, "The Valley," where Cher's party was, must have taken Josh hours to pick her up from.

On this particular trip, Cher herself, better known as Alicia Silverstone, was on our docket of people to interview. Nineties kids that we are, we were convinced Alicia would show up in a yellow plaid skirt suit sounding off "As if" the second we mentioned the traffic. We've found similar difficulty differentiating between Carrie Bradshaw and Sarah Jessica Parker. Turns out, trying to compare Cher and Alicia is as useless as searching for meaning in a Pauly Shore movie.

Cher had tried a number of diets, ranging from cutting her food into tiny little pieces to living off Special K, peanut M&M's, turkey bacon, and licorice. Alicia, though, was vegan. We were happy she'd found a lifestyle she could stick to.

We arrived at Gracias Madre—the plant-based Mexican restaurant Alicia had picked. Alicia walked in, and we weren't surprised to see that she had aged like Benjamin Button; if anything she had grown younger. She wore boyfriend jeans, flat sandals, and a '60s-esque Flower Power top of the bohemian persuasion. Very Cali, but not very Cher. She placed a recycled jar on the counter and asked the waiter to fill it up with water. Cher was a lot of things, but a friend to the environment was not one of them. We both subtly slipped our plastic Poland Spring bottles into our purses.

Alicia was a complete and total sweetheart, and as we photographed her with dishes like massaged kale with chipotle cashew dressing, guacamole tostadas, and mushroom-mole tacos, we chatted about motherhood and what made her decide to go vegan.

By the end of the shoot—after digging into all the dishes we photographed her with—we were nearly vegan converts ourselves.

Laura excused herself to go to the restroom and, as fate would have it, Alicia was getting up to go at the same time. It was one of those unbelievably awkward adult moments where two women who don't really know each other find themselves peeing next to each other in a two-stall bathroom.

Laura racked her brain upon entering. *Do I converse? Would that be crossing a boundary? Then again, if we don't converse, isn't it crossing a different boundary just listening to her pee?*

Luckily, Alicia brought some small talk to pass the time, but Laura was still out of that stall like a bull out of a gate. As they washed their hands, Laura went for the paper towels, doing that thing that only children do where they take one after the next after the next, until their mom says something like, "Do you really need that many paper towels?"

As Laura grabbed and chatted, she suddenly noticed Alicia was shaking her hands dry and staring at the paper towel dispenser.

Laura pondered what sort of pro-environmental plan she could make hoarding paper towels out to be . . . but she came up with nothing.

All in all, the shoot was a great success, but we'll never really know if Alicia Silverstone thinks of us as those two awesome girls from The New Potato, or those two environmentally irresponsible idiots. Potatoes are vegan, though, so that has to be working in our favor. . . .

Whether you're vegan, vegetarian, or neither at all, sometimes you just crave veggies. We promise even your meat-loving boyfriend/husband/best friend will like the veggie-centric mains coming up.

WARM ZUCCHINI NOODLE SALAD WITH PEANUT SAUCE

Serves 2 to 4

For the peanut sauce

¼ cup plus 2 tablespoons crunchy peanut butter

2 tablespoons fresh lime juice, plus lime wedges, for serving

2 tablespoons reduced-sodium soy sauce

1 tablespoon rice vinegar

1 teaspoon toasted sesame oil

1 teaspoon light brown sugar

1 teaspoon grated fresh ginger

1 small garlic clove, grated

1 teaspoon chili-garlic sauce

For the salad

Kosher salt

2 medium zucchini, spiralized (or 1 pound zucchini noodles)

2 medium carrots, spiralized (or 4 ounces shredded carrots)

4 ounces snow peas, sliced crosswise on the diagonal (about 1 cup)

2 scallions, thinly sliced

¼ cup cilantro leaves, roughly chopped, plus more for serving

¼ cup mint leaves, roughly chopped, plus more for serving

Chili-garlic sauce, for serving

One of our favorite things to order when we get Chinese takeout is cold sesame noodles. These are basically the same thing, but much healthier.

1.   **MAKE THE PEANUT SAUCE:** In a large bowl, whisk together the peanut butter, lime juice, soy sauce, vinegar, sesame oil, brown sugar, ginger, garlic, chili-garlic sauce, and 2 tablespoons water.

2.   **PREPARE THE SALAD:** In a large pot, bring salted water to a boil over high heat. Add the spiralized zucchini and cook until al dente, 1 to 2 minutes. Drain and shake off any excess water.

3.   Add the carrots, snow peas, scallions, and warm zucchini noodles to the dressing and toss. Add the cilantro and mint and toss again. Transfer to bowls and serve with more herbs, lime wedges, and chili-garlic sauce at the table.

NOTE: You can serve the zucchini noodles raw if you prefer. If heating them, be sure to cook until al dente and not past that! Serve right away so the sauce doesn't get watery.

LOADED SOUTHWEST SWEET POTATOES

Serves 4

4 medium sweet potatoes (about 8 ounces each)

3 tablespoons extra-virgin olive oil

1 medium red onion, diced

Kosher salt and freshly ground pepper

2 medium garlic cloves, thinly sliced

1 teaspoon ground cumin

1 pound kale, tough stems and central ribs removed, leaves roughly chopped

1 cup corn kernels, fresh (cut from 1 large ear) or frozen

1 (15-ounce) can black or pinto beans, drained and rinsed

Guacamole (recipe follows) or 1 avocado, sliced

½ cup cilantro leaves

1 large or 2 small radishes, cut into matchsticks

¼ cup toasted unsalted pumpkin seeds

We love, love, love sweet potatoes. They're the perfect snack, they satisfy sugar cravings, and they go with just about everything. You can follow this recipe (and it's good, so we suggest you do) or just load yours up with whatever you'd like.

1. Preheat the oven to 400°F.

2. Prick the potatoes in a few spots with a fork and arrange them on a baking sheet. Roast, turning once, until tender, about 40 minutes. Let cool slightly.

3. Meanwhile, in a large skillet, heat the olive oil over medium-high heat until warmed. Add the onion, season with salt and pepper, and cook until starting to soften, about 4 minutes. Add the garlic and cook until softened, about 2 minutes. Add the cumin and cook until fragrant, about 30 seconds. Add the kale and ¼ cup water and stir to coat. Cover and cook until the kale is wilted, about 5 minutes. Add more water as needed to prevent the bottom of the pan from scorching. Add the corn and beans and cook, stirring, until the beans are heated through and most of the liquid has evaporated, about 3 minutes. Season with salt and pepper.

4. Halve the sweet potatoes and arrange them cut side up on plates. Spoon the cooked vegetables on top. Dollop with the guacamole and sprinkle with cilantro, radishes, and pumpkin seeds.

Guacamole

Makes about 1 cup

1 Hass avocado

¼ cup diced tomato

1 tablespoon minced red onion

1½ tablespoons fresh lemon juice

1 tablespoon roughly chopped cilantro

¼ teaspoon kosher salt

In a medium bowl, use a fork to mash
the avocado so just a few chunks remain.
Fold in the tomato, onion, lemon juice,
cilantro, and salt. Serve.

BIBIMBAP

Serves 4

1 cup short-grain brown rice

1 tablespoon rice vinegar

1 teaspoon sugar

2 cups shredded carrots (or 4 ounces carrots, sliced into matchsticks)

Kosher salt

4 tablespoons neutral oil, plus more as needed

1 pound shiitake mushrooms, stems discarded and caps sliced (or 12 ounces presliced)

2 teaspoons reduced-sodium soy sauce

1 tablespoon minced garlic

1 (5-ounce) container greens, such as baby kale or spinach

½ teaspoon toasted sesame oil

1 cup kimchi

4 eggs

Thinly sliced scallion greens (optional)

Gochujang or other chile sauce

It looks like a lot of ingredients, but this recipe—our play on bibimbap—actually comes together quickly. It only requires one skillet plus a pot for cooking the rice. We love the mix of textures and flavors here: crunchy quick-pickled carrots; warm cooked mushrooms and greens; spicy kimchi; and of course, a runny egg. After you serve, use a spoon to break the egg yolks and stir everything together.

1. In a small pot, combine the rice and 1¾ cups water and bring to a boil over high heat. Cover and simmer over low heat until the water is absorbed and the rice is tender, about 45 minutes. Remove the pot from the heat and let stand, covered, for 5 minutes.

2. In a medium bowl, mix the vinegar with ½ teaspoon of the sugar until dissolved. Add the carrots, season with salt, and toss. Let stand while you prepare everything else.

3. In a large nonstick skillet, heat 1 tablespoon of the neutral oil over medium-high heat until warmed. Add the mushrooms, season lightly with salt, and cook, stirring, until softened and browned, about 8 minutes. Remove the skillet from the heat, add the soy sauce and the remaining ½ teaspoon sugar, and use the residual heat in the pan to cook until most of the liquid has evaporated. Scrape the mushrooms into a bowl and wipe out the skillet.

4. Add 1 tablespoon of the neutral oil and the garlic to the skillet and cook over medium heat until softened, about 1 minute. Add the greens and a few drops of water. Cook, stirring, until wilted, about 2 minutes. Drizzle the sesame oil over the greens and transfer the greens to the bowl with the mushrooms, keeping them in separate piles as much as possible. Wipe out the skillet again and remove from the heat.

5. Divide the rice among four bowls and top with piles of the carrots, mushrooms, greens, and kimchi.

6. In the same skillet, heat the remaining 2 tablespoons neutral oil over medium-high heat until shimmering. Crack 2 eggs into the skillet. After the edges of the egg whites are set, tip the skillet and spoon the oil that pools at the edge over the center of the eggs. When the egg whites are completely set but the yolk is still runny, transfer the eggs to two of the bowls. Repeat with the remaining eggs, adding more oil if needed.

7. Garnish the bibimbap with scallions (if using) and serve with gochujang alongside.

SPAGHETTI SQUASH PRIMAVERA

Serves 2 to 4

1 medium spaghetti squash (1½ to 2 pounds), halved lengthwise and seeded

4 tablespoons extra-virgin olive oil

Kosher salt and freshly ground black pepper

¼ pound green beans, sliced crosswise on the diagonal into 1-inch lengths

1 bunch of broccolini (about ¾ pound), cut into bite-size pieces

1 large garlic clove, sliced

¼ cup grated Pecorino Romano cheese, plus more for serving

Large pinch of crushed red pepper

This is a great alternative when you feel like you don't want to make pasta but still want something that satisfies that craving.

1.   Preheat the oven to 400°F.

2.   Arrange the squash halves cut side up on a baking sheet and brush with 2 tablespoons of the olive oil. Season with salt and black pepper. Turn cut side down and bake until tender, 30 to 40 minutes. Let cool until just warm.

3.   Meanwhile, in a large, deep skillet, heat the remaining 2 tablespoons olive oil over medium-high heat until shimmering. Add the green beans and broccolini and season with salt and pepper. Cook, stirring, until bright green, about 2 minutes. Add the garlic and cook until fragrant and softened, about 2 minutes. Add ¼ cup water, cover, and cook over medium heat until the vegetables are tender, 4 to 6 minutes.

4.   Using a fork, rake the warm spaghetti squash into threads and transfer to the skillet. Add the pecorino and cook until melted. Season with salt and black pepper and the crushed red pepper. Transfer the primavera to bowls and serve, passing more cheese at the table.

SOBA WITH EDAMAME, BROCCOLI, AND MISO DRESSING

Serves 2 to 4

Kosher salt

2 tablespoons fresh lemon juice

2 tablespoons rice vinegar

1 tablespoon miso

1 tablespoon reduced-sodium soy sauce

1 tablespoon toasted sesame oil

¼ cup neutral oil

2 teaspoons light brown sugar

3 scallions, chopped, white and
green parts separated

1 teaspoon finely grated fresh ginger

6 ounces soba noodles

3 cups broccoli florets (about 5 ounces)

1 cup shelled edamame

MAKE AHEAD: *The noodle salad can be refrigerated for several hours.*

1. Bring a large pot of salted water to a boil.

2. In a large bowl, whisk together the lemon juice, rice vinegar, miso, soy sauce, sesame oil, neutral oil, and brown sugar. Whisk in the scallion whites and ginger.

3. Add the soba to the pot and cook for 1 minute. Add the broccoli to the pot with the soba and cook for 2 minutes. Add the edamame and cook everything for 1 minute longer. Drain the noodles and vegetables. For a cool salad, run the noodles and vegetables under cold water, then drain well.

4. Add the hot or cooled noodles and vegetables to the dressing and toss. Add the scallion greens, toss again, and serve.

SMOKY CAULIFLOWER STEAKS WITH LEMON

Makes 2 steaks

1 medium head cauliflower
(about 2 pounds)

5 tablespoons extra-virgin olive oil

Kosher salt and freshly ground pepper

1 tablespoon fresh lemon juice

½ teaspoon smoked paprika

Toasted almonds and chopped parsley
(optional), for garnish

When you cut cauliflower steaks, you are inevitably left with excess cauliflower, perfect for making Cauliflower Couscous (page 181)!

1.   Preheat the oven to 425°F. When the oven is hot, preheat a large cast-iron skillet or other large ovenproof skillet in the oven for 5 minutes.

2.   Using a sharp knife, remove two of the rounded sides of the cauliflower, then cut the cauliflower lengthwise through the core to get 2 steaks, each about 1 inch thick. Reserve the remaining cauliflower for another use.

3.   Brush the cauliflower with 2 tablespoons of the olive oil and season with salt and pepper. Brush the preheated skillet lightly with 1 tablespoon of the oil and add the cauliflower steaks. (Reserve the brush.) Return to the oven and roast the steaks until the bottoms are starting to brown, about 10 minutes. Flip the steaks and roast until nearly tender, about 10 minutes longer.

4.   Meanwhile, in a small bowl, use the brush to mix together the lemon juice, smoked paprika, a pinch of salt, and the remaining 2 tablespoons olive oil.

5.   Brush the steaks on both sides with the smoky lemon sauce and roast until they are completely tender and are nicely browned, about 5 minutes longer.

6.   Remove the skillet from the oven and let the steaks rest in the skillet for 3 minutes, then transfer to plates. If desired, garnish with almonds and parsley and serve.

IT ALL STARTED WITH CARBONARA

*G*irl crushes don't necessarily only come along once in a lifetime, but we believe the truly great ones are few and far between. And when a mutual girl crush becomes a friendship . . . you can't ask for much more than that. It all started with carbonara. That is, a bowl of carbonara, a glass of white wine, and an unknown chic blonde with a stack of fashion magazines sporting Isabel Marant sneakers, an oversized white men's button-down, and an Acne Studios shearling coat.

PASTA WITH SALSA CRUDA AND BURRATA

Serves 4 to 6

Kosher salt

1 pound tomatoes

2 garlic cloves

2 tablespoons extra-virgin olive oil

Freshly ground pepper

12 ounces spaghetti or fettuccine

6 to 8 ounces burrata

Torn basil leaves, for garnish

This is possibly the perfect pasta. The burrata (is there anything better?) creates a light tomato cream sauce that feels really elevated, even though it's super-simple. If you prefer your sauce not-creamy, toss the pasta with the tomato sauce, transfer to bowls, and put the torn burrata on top. We're going to insist you try it our way at least once, though.

1. Bring a large pot of salted water to a boil over high heat.

2. Meanwhile, halve the tomatoes. Squeeze out as many of the seeds as possible and discard. Using a box grater, grate the tomato flesh on the large holes into a large bowl to form a puree. Stop when you reach the tomato skin. (For a chunkier sauce, you can chop up the tomato flesh instead.)

3. Smash the garlic cloves with the side of a knife and add to the grated tomatoes. Add the olive oil and season with salt and pepper. Let stand while you cook the pasta.

4. Add the pasta to the boiling water and cook according to the package directions, until al dente. Drain, shaking off any excess water.

5. Pick the garlic cloves out of the sauce and discard. Transfer the pasta to the bowl and toss. Season with salt and pepper. Use your fingers to pull apart the burrata and add it in large chunks, then toss the pasta again. Transfer the pasta to bowls, garnish with basil, and serve.

PIZZA MACARONI AND CHEESE

Serves 6 to 8

3 tablespoons unsalted butter, plus
more for the pan

Kosher salt

3 tablespoons all-purpose flour

2½ cups half-and-half

1 pound sharp white cheddar cheese,
shredded or cut into small pieces

½ pound low-moisture mozzarella
cheese, shredded or cut into small pieces

1 pound elbow macaroni or other short
pasta shape, such as penne

1½ cups tomato puree

½ teaspoon dried oregano

1 large garlic clove, grated

2 tablespoons extra-virgin olive oil

½ pound fresh mozzarella,
torn into small pieces

Grated Parmigiano-Reggiano cheese
and basil leaves, for garnish

This is exactly as awesome as it sounds. Although we've never been big classic mac 'n' cheese fans, we do have a great affinity for baked ziti, pizza, and the like, which is how this amazing recipe was born.

1. Preheat the oven to 350°F. Butter a 12-inch cast-iron skillet or any shallow 2-quart ovenproof dish.

2. Bring a large pot of salted water to a boil over high heat.

3. In a large saucepan, melt the butter over medium heat. Add the flour and cook to form a paste, about 2 minutes. Add the half-and-half and whisk constantly until the sauce is thickened, about 5 minutes. Remove the pot from the heat and add half of the cheddar and low-moisture mozzarella. Stir gently until melted, returning the pot to low heat to melt completely if necessary.

4. Add the macaroni to the boiling water and cook until barely cooked through. Drain the macaroni and return it to the pot. Add the cheese sauce. Stir in the remaining cheddar and low-moisture mozzarella; don't worry if the cheeses don't melt completely.

5. Spread the macaroni in the prepared skillet or baking dish and bake until bubbling, about 25 minutes.

6. Meanwhile, in a small saucepan, combine the tomato puree, oregano, garlic, and olive oil and season with salt. Simmer over medium heat for 5 minutes, just until the flavors meld.

7. Spread the tomato sauce on top of the macaroni and cheese, leaving a ½-inch border. Arrange the pieces of fresh mozzarella on top and bake until the fresh mozzarella is melted, 10 to 15 minutes longer.

8. To serve, sprinkle shredded Parmesan on top and garnish with basil leaves.

DEATH OF A (CENTRAL PARK) SALESMAN

*W*e are tried-and-true theater nerds at heart. It was a hobby of Danielle's that Laura took up soon thereafter (in typical younger sister fashion). There are boxes upon boxes of plays gathering dust in our parents' attic, and we've read every one. Some suburban high schoolers took advantage of weekends and their proximity to New York City by taking the train in and drinking beers and smoking pot in Central Park. We got even crazier—we'd take that train in and camp out at the Drama Book Shop on West 40th Street.

It was no surprise, then, that Laura's first summer internship was in marketing at the Public Theater. She worked at their location in Central Park, the Delacorte Theater, where the Public put on two plays each summer (usually Shakespeare), each running for about six weeks. The plays that summer were *Romeo and Juliet* and *A Midsummer Night's Dream*.

Our whole family went to dinner in Little Italy to celebrate Laura's first internship as a big-time theater marketing professional. We were at our family mainstay for celebrations, Angelo's, and our table was loaded with Bolognese, ragù, and chicken Parmesan . . . the dinner of champions. Every Kosann celebration happened at Angelo's, whether a birthday, an anniversary, or even something as unmonumental as one of us scoring a goal in a soccer game. The Kosanns have always used any and every excuse to celebrate over food, and that particular night Danielle toasted to the promise and cachet associated with the Delacorte Theater.

"You do know Meryl Streep and Kevin Kline did Chekhov there in 2001," Danielle said, glass raised.

"No way! *The Cherry Orchard*?" Laura asked.

"*The Seagull*," Danielle said, nodding knowingly.

"Stop. I can't even."

Our parents took sips of their wine. We're not sure if they were proud, or worried.

On her first day, Laura entered the theater via Central Park with a spring in her step and a coffee in her hand.

I'm a true New York working girl, she thought, and her mind went straight to the opening montage of *The Devil Wears Prada*. She was intimidated; but remembering her high school experience working as a sales associate at the Ralph Lauren store in town, she knew she was well equipped for any marketing challenges this job would throw her way.

Upon entering, Laura was shocked to see how tiny the office was. It was the inside of the space where people walked up to get tickets and merchandise, and before Laura could react . . .

"Ah! You're here, just in time," Karen, the woman who had interviewed Laura, said upon opening the door. "I'm almost done filling this up."

She had a cart full of T-shirts, sweatshirts, mugs, and baseball caps with Public Theater logos on them. Laura looked up. "Just in time?"

"So you see that line out there?" Karen continued. "That's where people wait for their free tickets. They come as early as five a.m. so the line goes way, way back. Here's your cart!"

"You want me to push the cart out there and sell this stuff, you mean?" The *Devil Wears Prada* montage began to fade.

"Uh-huh . . . Just skip that guy at the front, though. That's Space Pussy," she said, pointing to a sleeping homeless guy at the front of the line who was wearing a ripped T-shirt with a cat on it.

"Space . . . Pussy?"

"Yeah, Space Pussy. He's here every day."

Laura considered sharing the maxim she learned at Ralph Lauren—that *every* customer matters, especially a consistent one like Space Pussy—but she thought better of it.

"I'm sure he scalps the tickets," Karen sighed. Then she turned back to the pile of tickets she was counting up.

"Okay . . . I'll just take this, then."

Laura grabbed the cart and walked outside.

A text from Danielle came through: "So?! Are they rehearsing?"

Laura hung her head in shame and wrote back: "Did you know the tickets here are free?"

DANIELLE: Of course, it's theater for the people. Hence PUBLIC Theater.

LAURA: So what'd you think the marketing part of this job was going to be?

DANIELLE: I dunno . . . I didn't really think about it. . . . What is it?

LAURA: Selling T-shirts.

DANIELLE: What do you mean?

LAURA: Exactly what it sounds like.

Danielle usually found a silver lining, so her silence wasn't a good sign. Laura made her way past Space Pussy, phone still in hand.

LAURA: This is ridiculous. Do I just walk by the line with the cart? Do I yell what I have like a hot dog vendor?

DANIELLE: You're the saleswoman. . . .

Laura approached a couple at the front of the line. "Do you guys want a Delacorte Theater hoodie, or maybe a mug? They're special edition for this season."

"How much is the hoodie?" A man in very short shorts asked testily.

"Um, forty-five dollars."

"Right, so we come and wait for four hours for free theater tickets, and we're going to spend forty-five dollars on a hoodie? I thought this was theater for the people."

Laura's Ralph Lauren experience had not prepared her for this. She continued along with her cart. By the third day, though, Laura got the hang of it. In fact, in her typical competitive type A fashion, she came back from the line with a $500 wad of cash. Karen nearly had a heart attack.

"Switch to the production internship there next summer," Danielle advised. "That's bound to be more theater-centric."

So switch Laura did, and though she was able to watch rehearsals on her downtime, the rest of her time was allotted to quite a different task. The plays that year were *Hamlet* and *Hair;* the set of *Hair* had grass covering the entirety of the stage. The interns were assigned to cut the grass down with tiny scissors all summer, which is like asking someone to groom your lawn with arts and crafts scissors rather than mow it.

When Laura brought Danielle to the opening night, Danielle was ecstatic. And at intermission Danielle raved, "'Aquarius' was awesome! I love the sixties-era costumes; they didn't go too over the top. And that number right before intermission was so powerful."

"Totally," Laura said. Then, after a pause: "How do you think the grass looked?"

Despite the fact that Laura didn't make a career out of this internship, it was still worth celebrating at Angelo's—most importantly, for more pasta.

ORECCHIETTE WITH SAUSAGE, BROCCOLI RABE, AND RICOTTA

Serves 4 to 6

Kosher salt

1 pound sweet or hot Italian sausage, casings removed

2 tablespoons extra-virgin olive oil

2 garlic cloves, thinly sliced

1 large bunch broccoli rabe (about 1 pound), coarsely chopped

12 ounces orecchiette

¼ cup freshly grated Parmigiano-Reggiano cheese

1 cup fresh ricotta cheese

Hands down, this is one of our all-time favorite pasta combinations. We're not going to pretend we invented it, but we *have* mastered making it at home. The key is to get the sausage really broken up so that it mixes with the cheese and really coats the pasta.

1. Bring a large pot of salted water to a boil over high heat.

2. Meanwhile, in a large skillet, cook the sausage over medium heat, using a spoon to break up the meat into small pieces, until cooked through, about 8 minutes. Transfer the sausage to a plate.

3. Add the olive oil and garlic to the skillet and cook until the garlic is softened, about 2 minutes. Add ¼ cup water and scrape up any browned bits from the bottom of the skillet. Add the broccoli rabe, cover, and cook until the greens are just wilted, about 2 minutes. Uncover, increase the heat to medium-high, and cook until the greens are very soft and most of the liquid has evaporated, about 5 minutes.

4. Add the orecchiette to the boiling water and cook according to the package directions, until al dente. Reserving ½ cup of the pasta cooking water, drain the pasta and transfer to the skillet.

5. Return the sausage to the skillet and cook over medium heat, stirring until everything is incorporated and hot and adding a little pasta water as needed to loosen the sauce. Stir in the Parmesan. Divide the pasta among bowls, top with a dollop of ricotta, and serve.

LAMB SHANK RAGÙ

Serves 4 to 6

3 tablespoons extra-virgin olive oil

2 lamb shanks (about 1¾ pounds)

1 medium onion, diced

2 medium carrots, diced

Kosher salt and freshly ground pepper

1 teaspoon fennel seeds

1 teaspoon ground coriander

½ teaspoon ground cumin

1 cup dry red wine

1 (28-ounce) can whole tomatoes
with juices

10 pitted green olives, sliced into rounds

12 ounces tagliatelle

Grated Parmigiano-Reggiano cheese,
for serving

MAKE AHEAD: *The sauce can be refrigerated for up to 3 days or frozen for up to 2 months.*

This ragù is full and flavorful, due in part to the fact that you simmer the lamb shanks for 2 hours in the sauce, until they're super-tender.

1. In a Dutch oven or enameled cast-iron casserole, heat the olive oil over medium-high heat until shimmering. Add the lamb shanks and cook, turning, until browned all over, about 8 minutes. Transfer to a plate.

2. Add the onion and carrots to the pot, season with salt and pepper, and cook over medium heat, stirring occasionally, until tender, about 8 minutes. Add the fennel seeds, coriander, and cumin and toast, stirring constantly, until fragrant, about 30 seconds. Add the wine, bring to a boil, and simmer on low heat until reduced by half, about 15 minutes. Add the tomatoes with their juices and use a spoon to break them up into pieces. Return to a boil, then reduce the heat to medium-low.

3. Return the lamb shanks to the pot and cover with a piece of parchment paper cut to fit the top of the pot, followed by the lid. Simmer the lamb shanks until very tender, about 2 hours. Remove the shanks from the pot and pull the meat into bite-size pieces. Return the meat to the sauce and add the sliced olives.

4. Bring a large pot of salted water to a boil over high heat. Add the tagliatelle and cook according to the package directions, until al dente. Drain and add the pasta to the ragù and toss. Season with more salt and pepper if needed. Serve, passing Parmesan at the table.

MUSHROOM BOLOGNESE

Serves 6 to 8

1 small onion, chopped

2 small carrots, chopped

1 celery rib, chopped

1 pound white or cremini mushrooms

½ pound shiitake mushrooms, stems discarded

¼ cup extra-virgin olive oil

Kosher salt and freshly ground pepper

3 garlic cloves, minced

2 tablespoons tomato paste

1 sprig sage

1 sprig rosemary

1 sprig basil

1 cup dry red wine

1 (28-ounce) can crushed tomatoes

1 cup whole milk

1 Parmigiano-Reggiano cheese rind

1½ pounds spaghetti

Grated Parmigiano-Reggiano cheese, for serving

MAKE AHEAD: *The sauce can be refrigerated for up to 3 days and frozen for up to 3 months.*

We cannot speak highly enough of this dish. You will never, ever need to make beef Bolognese again. This recipe makes about 5 cups of sauce, so sometimes we like to use half (and only 12 ounces of pasta) and freeze the rest for another day. It's also great over polenta. The sauce simmers for 1 hour 20 minutes.

1. In a food processor, pulse together the onion, carrots, celery, and both mushrooms until finely chopped, working in batches if necessary.

2. In a large pot, heat the olive oil over medium heat until warmed. Add the vegetables, season with salt and pepper, and cook, stirring occasionally, until softened, about 15 minutes. Add the garlic and cook until softened, about 3 minutes. Add the tomato paste and herbs and cook, stirring, until the paste glazes the bottom of the pan, about 2 minutes.

3. Add the wine, bring to a boil over high heat, and cook until reduced by half, about 3 minutes. Add the crushed tomatoes, milk, and Parmesan rind and use your spoon to break up the tomatoes a bit. Reduce the heat to medium-low and simmer, partly covered, until the flavors develop and the sauce is a little glossy, about 1 hour 20 minutes. Discard the cheese rind and herbs and season with salt and pepper.

4. Meanwhile, bring a large pot of salted water to a boil over high heat.

5. Add the spaghetti and cook according to the package directions, until al dente. Reserving about 1 cup of the pasta cooking water, drain the pasta and add to the sauce. Toss, adding a little pasta water as needed to loosen the sauce. Serve with grated Parmesan passed at the table.

IN THE EARLY DAYS OF THE WEBSITE, WE WERE DETERMINED TO MAKE KRIS JENNER INTO WHAT WE WERE CALLING A POTATOHEAD—A HUGE FAN AND FOLLOWER OF THE NEW POTATO. WE THOUGHT MAYBE KOURTNEY, KHLOÉ, KIM, AND KANYE WOULD ALL FOLLOW IN HER FOOTSTEPS.

KEEPING UP WITH KRIS JENNER

On the day of our interview, Kris wanted to meet at one of her favorite food spots, Nobu Malibu, which is an unbelievable space right on the water. We were staying at what had become our West Coast home, Sunset Tower Hotel, and already knew we had to provide ample time for the drive.

We weren't too worried, though: This was Kris Jenner—what were the chances she was showing up on time? We'd had experience shooting celebrities and learned that most often the agreed-upon start time was a loose promise. Eleven a.m. meant twelve, five p.m. meant six-thirty. As a result we came to know the full life story of every publicist with whom we found ourselves whiling away the hours at the front of a restaurant.

So you can imagine our shock at getting an email thirty-five minutes before the Nobu shoot from Kris's team saying something like "We're here! Are you close? She's around the corner!"

Crap. We were *in* Malibu, but we'd passed the restaurant to pick up some iced coffee at the Coffee Bean.

Still newbies to West Coast driving, our missing a destination on a large avenue had become an everyday occurrence, and this was no exception. It was always the same process: We had to recalibrate, attempt five left turns before finding a legal one; and once we finally turned around, we always seemed to enter the one-way exit in a parking lot rather than the entrance. While drivers in LA don't have the road rage we New Yorkers do, they have a passive-aggressive attitude, which can be even worse. They shake their heads and push up their Ray-Bans just long enough to give a look that seems to say *New Yorkers, right?* Then they finally reverse so you can enter.

This time, though, we didn't have time for failed left-turn attempts. Instead, Danielle put the pedal to the metal and made the U-turn heard round the world. The way this scene looks in our heads is something out of *The Fast and the Furious;* the way it actually looked was that scene in *Clueless* where Dionne accidentally gets on the freeway.

Kris's publicist had mentioned the risk of paparazzi following Kris to the shoot, and while we of course acted hopeful they wouldn't, the entirety of our conversation on the way to Malibu was about how cool it would be if they did. We debated the possible headlines:

"Kris Jenner Sighting: Epic Shoot with The New Potato."

"Kris Jenner Skips Out for a Shoot with Two Beautiful Mystery Women."

"Who Wore It Best? The New Potato's Laura Kosann or Jessica Biel?"

Luckily, we arrived right before Kris, but to our dismay there were no paparazzi in sight.

"Thank goodness," the press rep said. "They usually come to the beach for something on the water like this." We nodded, miming looks of "relief."

When Kris walked in, it seemed there was no discrepancy between who she was in real life and who she was on *Keeping Up with the Kardashians.* We suppose that's the whole premise of the reality TV industry, huh?

We set her up for our shoot at a table overlooking the beach, accompanied by edamame and water. She is a natural-born poser. The second Danielle lifted her camera, Kris sprang into action: laugh pose, happy pose, *The Thinker* pose, look-away pose, tilt-your-head-back pose, nibble-edamame pose. They were all there, and she moved through them seamlessly.

At a certain point Kris said something like, "Okay, I'm done. You got it." Danielle recognized that there was no such thing as disagreeing in

this circumstance and immediately responded, "Um, yes, right, I got it."

As we were leaving, the publicist said to Kris, "Kanye wants you to call him right away!" We looked at each other like two kids at Christmas.

Laura's eyes widened: *Kanye?!?!*

Danielle cocked her head: *How can we get him here?*

Laura crossed her arms: *Now that's a headline.*

Danielle cocked an eyebrow: *Do you think it'd be weird if we stayed and ordered some sashimi?*

Laura scratched her head: *You lost me.*

In the end, though, there was nary a paparazzo in sight, and Kanye never came. We didn't even get sashimi.

Being in Los Angeles always makes us crave seafood—from lobster tacos at Sunset Tower to sashimi at Nobu Malibu to absolutely anything on the menu at Son of a Gun. But seafood can be sort of daunting to make at home. We're here to tell you that actually it's not. At least, not when you have the right recipes.

SHRIMP AND POTATO CHIP ROLL

Makes 4 sandwiches

1 lemon, sliced, plus 1 teaspoon fresh
lemon juice

1 pound large shrimp, peeled
and deveined

1 tablespoon mayonnaise

Kosher salt and freshly ground pepper

4 hot dog buns, toasted

Large handful of potato chips of choice

When we were kids, there was absolutely no
way to eat a potato chip other than to put it on a
sandwich. PB&J, turkey, tuna salad . . . whatever
it was, potato chips (Cape Cod, if you must know)
were always added for the final touch. This shrimp
roll is easy to make, but we insist that it will not be
the same without those potato chips tucked inside.

1. Fill a large pot with water, add the lemon
slices, and bring to a boil over high heat. Add the
shrimp and cook until opaque throughout, 1 to 2
minutes. Drain, discarding the lemon, and run the
shrimp under cold water. Chop into bite-size pieces.

2. In a large bowl, toss the shrimp with the
mayonnaise and lemon juice. Season with salt and
pepper. Pile the shrimp salad into the toasted buns
and tuck in some potato chips as well. Serve.

LOBSTER–RICE NOODLE SALAD WITH COCONUT MILK DRESSING

Serves 4

1 (1½-pound) live lobster

4 ounces rice stick noodles

⅓ cup canned full-fat coconut milk

1 tablespoon fish sauce

1 tablespoon fresh lime juice, plus lime wedges, for serving

1 tablespoon dark brown sugar

1 small garlic clove, minced

1 teaspoon sambal oelek, plus more to taste and for serving

½ cup carrot matchsticks (about 2 ounces)

5 ounces cucumbers, cut into 2-inch-long wedges

½ cup cilantro, roughly chopped

¼ cup mint leaves, roughly chopped

¼ cup fresh Thai basil leaves, roughly chopped

2 tablespoons roughly chopped unsalted roasted peanuts (optional)

MAKE AHEAD: *The chopped lobster meat, the dressing, and the prepped vegetables can be refrigerated in separate airtight containers overnight.*

We would never dare attempt to replicate (and probably ruin) the Sunset Tower lobster tacos, so we usually stick to this recipe instead. It's nice for lunch or dinner, particularly in spring/summer. If you're not a lobster fan, you could make this with 1 pound shrimp, peeled, or 1 chicken breast half, chopped. You can also buy precooked/prechopped lobster.

1. Bring a large stockpot of water to a boil over high heat. Plunge the lobster into the pot headfirst and boil for 12 minutes. Using tongs, transfer to a baking sheet and let cool.

2. While the lobster cools, prepare the noodles according to the package directions. Drain and run under cold water, then shake to drain well.

3. Separate the lobster claws and tail from the head (discard the head shell or reserve for stock). Use scissors to snip up the center of the underside of the lobster tail. Pull the tail apart and remove the meat from the shell in one piece. Halve the tail lengthwise and remove the intestinal veins. Use the bottom of a knife to crack the claws and remove the meat. Chop all of the lobster meat into small bite-size pieces. (You should have about 1⅓ cups.)

4. In a large bowl, whisk together the coconut milk, fish sauce, lime juice, and brown sugar until the sugar dissolves. Stir in the garlic and sambal. Taste and add more sambal if you like more heat.

5. Add the noodles, carrots, and cucumbers to the dressing and toss. Add the lobster and herbs and toss again. Taste for seasoning, sprinkle with the peanuts (if using), and serve with lime wedges and more sambal on the side.

CLAMS with POTATOES, CORN, and BASIL

Serves 4

½ pound baby potatoes

2 small to medium ears of corn, husked
(or 2 cups frozen corn kernels)

3 tablespoons extra-virgin olive oil
or unsalted butter

1 leek, halved, sliced, and cleaned
(see Note)

Kosher salt and freshly ground pepper

1 cup dry white wine

3 dozen littleneck clams, scrubbed

Torn fresh basil leaves, for serving

NOTE: *Leeks are full of grit, so you need to clean them well. First trim off the root and the dark green tops. Halve the leek lengthwise, then thinly slice crosswise. Rinse the slices under cold running water.*

We used to be afraid to make clams at home, but discovering this recipe has totally turned us. It brings together some classic chowder ingredients without the creamy soup base and is excellent for a summer night with a bottle of chilled rosé.

1. In a large pot, cover the potatoes with water and bring to a boil over medium-high heat. Simmer until tender, 10 to 15 minutes. Drain and let cool, then slice the potatoes into coins.

2. Using a serrated knife, with an ear of corn set in a bowl, slice down the cob to remove the kernels. Repeat with the other ear.

3. In the same pot, heat the olive oil over medium heat until warmed. Add the leek, season lightly with salt and pepper, and cook until softened, about 5 minutes. Add the wine, increase the heat to medium-high, bring to a boil, and cook for 1 minute to cook off most of the alcohol. Add the clams and cover the pot. Cook until the clams open, about 5 minutes. As the clams open, transfer them to a large bowl. Discard any clams that do not open after 10 minutes.

4. Slowly pour the clam broth into another bowl, leaving behind the last few tablespoons, which may contain a little sand. Rinse out the pot and return it to the heat.

5. Return the broth to the pot. Add the potatoes and corn to the pot and cook until the vegetables are heated through and the broth is slightly thickened, about 2 minutes.

6. Arrange the clams in bowls and ladle the vegetables and broth on top. Garnish with basil and serve.

SIMPLE BRANZINO WITH ROASTED GARLIC DRESSING

Serves 2 to 4

2 whole branzino (1 to 1½ pounds each), gutted and scaled

¼ cup plus 2 tablespoons extra-virgin olive oil, plus more for brushing

Kosher salt and freshly ground pepper

1 lemon, sliced into rounds, plus 2 tablespoons fresh lemon juice

10 sprigs flat-leaf parsley, plus ¼ cup finely chopped parsley

3 small to medium garlic cloves, unpeeled

Roasting a whole fish always feels pretty baller to us. Branzino is one of our favorites—it makes us feel like we're dining on a beach on the Italian coast. Ask your fishmonger to gut and scale the fish.

1. Preheat the oven to 425°F. Line a baking sheet with parchment paper.

2. Brush the branzino all over with olive oil and season with salt and pepper. Arrange the fish on the baking sheet and stuff the cavities with the lemon rounds and parsley sprigs. Brush the garlic cloves with a little oil and arrange them on the baking sheet as well. Roast the fish until the flesh is opaque and pulls easily away from the backbone, 15 to 20 minutes. Transfer to a platter.

3. Squeeze the roasted garlic from the skins into a medium bowl and use a fork to mash. Add the lemon juice and ¼ cup plus 2 tablespoons olive oil. Mix in the chopped parsley. Season with salt and pepper and serve alongside the fish.

TERIYAKI SALMON RICE BOWLS WITH CUCUMBER AND AVOCADO

Serves 4

2 tablespoons neutral oil

2 garlic cloves, minced

1 tablespoon grated fresh ginger
(from about 1 inch)

1 cup short-grain brown or black rice

¼ cup reduced-sodium soy sauce

2 tablespoons honey

2 tablespoons rice vinegar

1 teaspoon toasted sesame oil

4 (6-ounce) salmon fillets

Kosher salt

3 mini (Persian) cucumbers, thinly sliced

1 Hass avocado, thinly sliced

Toasted sesame seeds and sliced scallion
greens (optional), for garnish

This is a go-to weeknight recipe for us. It gets us out of the "piece of salmon with a boring side" rut.

1. In a small pot, heat 1 tablespoon of the neutral oil over medium heat until warmed. Add the garlic and ginger and cook until fragrant and softened, about 1 minute. Add the rice and 1¾ cups water, cover, and cook until the rice is tender and the water is absorbed, about 45 minutes. Remove the pot from the heat and let the rice stand, covered, for 5 minutes.

2. Meanwhile, in a small bowl, whisk together the soy sauce, honey, rice vinegar, and sesame oil. Set the teriyaki sauce aside.

3. About 15 minutes before the rice is done, in a large skillet, heat the remaining 1 tablespoon neutral oil over medium-high heat until shimmering. Season the salmon lightly with salt and add to the pan skin side down. Cook until the skin is browned and crisp, about 4 minutes. Flip and cook for 1 minute, so the fish is not yet cooked through. Transfer to a plate.

4. Pour the oil out of the skillet and wipe it clean. Add the teriyaki sauce and bring to a boil over medium-high heat. Cook until the sauce is reduced by half, about 1 minute. Return the salmon to the skillet, skin side up. Tip the skillet so the sauce pools and spoon it over the salmon and cook until the sauce is syrupy and the salmon is just cooked through, about 2 minutes. Remove the skillet from the heat.

5. Fluff the rice and divide among four bowls. Top with the salmon, cucumber slices, and avocado. Serve, garnished with sesame seeds and scallion greens if desired.

TO VIENNA WITH LOVE

*T*here's no version of *What to Expect When You're Expecting* *when it comes to going on a weeklong trip to Europe with your grandparents. You throw the dice and figure either you'll have an incredible time or the whole thing will unravel like a Noël Coward play.*

Grandmommy wanted to take us to Vienna over Christmas to show us where she grew up. She had written an incredible book about her childhood and surviving the Holocaust; the plan was to see all the different people and places she'd written about. It was an amazing trip.

To say Grandmommy began planning early is a bit of an understatement. We were set to leave on December 23, but it was around September 23 that she called us to let us know what time the car was picking us up at the airport:

"So it will be a black car from the hotel . . . Hotel Bristol . . . it will say it on the car! When you get off the plane the driver will be waiting for you. Once you're off the plane, please call my cell phone."

"We'll also talk closer to then to finalize the plan, right?" Danielle asked.

"Yes, Danieli. So call me on my cell phone *right* when you arrive at the airport."

Yes, in three months, we'd call her on her cell phone *right* when we arrived at the airport.

It was a surprise Grandmommy gave such attention to detail on this matter given her madcap ways. These were especially prevalent when it came to cooking. When we were growing up, walking into her kitchen could be a bit like entering a very charming war zone: raw chicken lying on the countertop, white onions burning on the stove, and Lumpazi (short for Lumpazivagabundus)—her bird—squawking as she chopped.

And in her refrigerator, there was simply no such thing as an expiration date. She challenged the whole concept of expirations. None of her dinner party guests (that we know of) has ever gotten sick, yet the butter in there had been around since Nixon was impeached.

But when Grandmommy said a stick of butter from the '70s was fine, you simply had to agree with her. Whether something is so or not so, Grandmommy will make it so if that's her opinion on the matter. In fact, when our mom bought a dinner from an auction for Danielle's birthday that consisted of going to Anthony Bourdain's restaurant and sitting with Anthony himself, Grandmommy quizzed him:

"I recently tried a charming Greek restaurant called Milos," she said to Anthony across the table.

He smiled politely.

"Have you been to Milos?" she continued.

"Excuse me?" he asked, not hearing her.

A little bit louder now. "Have you been to MI-LOS?"

"I haven't actually," Anthony said.

"Aren't you in the food industry? My granddaughter tells me you are in the food industry, no?"

We both nearly ducked under the table to avoid being the granddaughter she was pointing at. Anthony Bourdain has yet to be on The New Potato.

The first funny challenge we faced upon arriving in Vienna was GPS . . . or lack thereof. We love getting lost in a city, but Grandmommy had very specific destinations in mind. She didn't know how to get to those destinations, but she also refused to look at a map.

"We will find it, we will find it," she'd exclaim, looking around.

We half expected her to lick her finger and hold it in the air to see which way the wind was blowing.

"I can check on my phone, Grandmommy. Should I just look at the map?" Laura would ask.

"No, no, we are fine, see I know it's there somewhere," she'd say, as she pointed across the river to the south side of the city. This narrowed things down.

Further drawing out our travels were Christkindlmarkets. They're the charming, outdoor traditional Christmas markets in Vienna that all boast the same exact souvenir, food, and tchotchke stands. Grandmommy insisted on walking through them *every* time we passed one. During Christmastime in Vienna that's a little like stopping at every Starbucks you pass in New York City.

But even while lost, we found that one of the best things about Vienna was eating our way through it with Grandmommy. When we went to Demel, one of the most famous Viennese cafés for pastry, Grandmommy ordered the entire pastry menu. This isn't an exaggeration. Minutes after we sat down, our entire table was covered in *Kaiserschmarrn,* apple strudel, *Marmorgugelhupf, Mohnbeugel, Nussbeugel* . . . the list goes on. And at night, we'd order supposedly single orders of Wiener schnitzel that in reality could feed families of four.

Two operas, five museums, forty-four Christkindlmarkets, and seven Wiener schnitzels later . . . it was our last day in Vienna, and Grandmommy wanted to get Sachertorte, a traditional Viennese chocolate cake, at the official Hotel Sacher. Unfortunately, the wait was a long one, so we suggested getting Sachertorte to go and eating it back at the hotel.

"No," Grandmommy said, as if we'd just suggested tampering with evidence. "I don't do Sacher-to-go."

It seemed like a hard-and-fast rule. So we waited and finally, after an hour, ended up sitting in the traditional Viennese café for this delicious chocolate cake with schlag (a.k.a. whipped cream) accompanied by espressos.

It was no Milos . . . but it was damn good Sachertorte.

Suffice it to say . . . we've learned how to make a damn good schnitzel. Grandmommy taught us that dinner is always an occasion, no matter where you are. We like to think she's where we get our knack for always making mealtime a celebration—even if it's just a simple roast chicken at home. Here are some recipes for poultry and meat.

EASY VEAL SCHNITZEL

Makes 4 small schnitzels

1 cup panko bread crumbs

1 teaspoon dried thyme

1 teaspoon onion powder

1 teaspoon sweet paprika

Kosher salt

1 egg, lightly beaten

1 teaspoon Dijon mustard

1 cup all-purpose flour

Neutral oil, for cooking

4 very thin veal cutlets
(2 to 3 ounces each)

Lemon wedges and New Potato Salad
(page 175), for serving

We don't typically eat veal, but for this we make an exception. It's worth making the potato salad and having that on the side—that's how we did it in Vienna!

1. In a medium shallow bowl or pie plate, toss together the panko, thyme, onion powder, paprika, and 1 teaspoon salt. In a second shallow bowl, beat together the egg and mustard with a fork. Place the flour in a third medium shallow bowl.

2. In a large skillet, heat about ¼ inch of oil over medium heat until a bread crumb bubbles briskly when added. Meanwhile, working quickly, dredge the cutlets through the flour and tap off any excess. Coat with the egg, allowing any excess to drip off. Finally, dredge the cutlets through the bread crumbs, pressing to adhere.

3. Working in batches if necessary, add the cutlets to the oil and cook until the bottoms are golden brown, about 2 minutes. Flip and cook until the crust is golden and the meat is cooked through, about 2 minutes longer.

4. Transfer the cutlets to paper towels to drain. Sprinkle lightly with salt, if desired, then serve immediately with lemon wedges and potato salad alongside.

GREEN CHICKEN CURRY

Serves 4

1 tablespoon neutral oil

1½ pounds boneless, skinless chicken breasts, cut into bite-size pieces

¾ pound zucchini, cut into bite-size pieces

6 ounces shiitake mushrooms, stems discarded, caps sliced (or 4 ounces presliced)

½ recipe Green Curry Paste (recipe follows)

1 (14-ounce) can full-fat coconut milk

2 tablespoons fish sauce

1 tablespoon light brown sugar

1 lime, plus lime wedges, for serving

Cilantro leaves, for garnish

Steamed rice, for serving

When we were kids, our mom made a lot of chicken. While we love chicken as much as the next person, it also can get old. But it's probably the easiest protein to just grab at the store and make quickly during the week. (We get it now, Mom!) As we've gotten older, we've sought out ways to make chicken a little more fun, and this is one of our favorites. The jalapeño seeds in the green curry paste are left in for spice, but leave them out if you like a milder curry.

1. In an enameled cast-iron casserole or Dutch oven, heat the oil over medium-high heat until shimmering. Add half the chicken and stir-fry until browned all over, about 3 minutes. Use a slotted spoon to transfer the chicken to a plate. Repeat with the remaining chicken, transferring to a plate.

2. Add the zucchini and mushrooms to the pot and stir-fry until barely tender, about 4 minutes. Add the curry paste and stir-fry for 1 minute. Add the coconut milk, fish sauce, and brown sugar, and bring to a boil. Using a vegetable peeler, remove 1 long strip of lime zest and add to the pot. Return the chicken to the pot and simmer until the chicken is cooked through, about 3 minutes. Halve the lime and squeeze in the juice. Ladle the curry into bowls and garnish with cilantro leaves. Serve on top of steamed rice with lime wedges, for squeezing.

Green Curry Paste
Serves 8

This recipe makes twice as much curry paste as is needed for the chicken curry, so use it in a stir-fry later in the week, as a spread for grilled cheese, or spooned over scrambled eggs.

1 stalk lemongrass or 1 tablespoon
    lemongrass paste

3 jalapeños, roughly chopped

3 garlic cloves, roughly chopped

2 inches fresh ginger, roughly chopped

1 medium shallot, roughly chopped

½ cup cilantro leaves

2 teaspoons ground coriander

½ teaspoon ground cumin

Grated zest and juice of 1 lime

1 tablespoon fish sauce

Remove the outer few layers of the lemongrass and the top several inches. Roughly chop the tender inner core and transfer to a food processor. Add the jalapeños, garlic, ginger, shallot, cilantro, coriander, cumin, lime zest, lime juice, and fish sauce and pulse until a paste forms.

LEMONY ROAST CHICKEN WITH POTATOES AND ONIONS

Serves 3 or 4

1½ pounds fingerling potatoes, preferably mixed colors, halved lengthwise or quartered if large

2 small onions, peeled and each cut into 8 wedges

4 garlic cloves, unpeeled

2 tablespoons extra-virgin olive oil

6 sprigs thyme

6 sprigs rosemary

Kosher salt and freshly ground pepper

2 tablespoons unsalted butter

1 whole chicken (about 4 pounds)

1 lemon, halved

1. Position a rack in the center of the oven and preheat to 425°F.

2. In a roasting pan, large cast-iron skillet, or rimmed baking sheet, toss the potatoes, onions, and garlic cloves with the olive oil and half of the herb sprigs. Season with salt and pepper.

3. Melt 1 tablespoon of the butter. Brush the chicken cavity with some of the butter and stuff with the lemon halves and remaining herb sprigs. Tie the legs together with kitchen string. Brush more melted butter all over the chicken and season with salt and pepper. Set the chicken in the center of the roasting pan (push the vegetables and potatoes to the side to make some room) and roast for 35 minutes.

4. Meanwhile, melt the remaining 1 tablespoon butter.

5. Brush the chicken all over with the melted butter. Rotate the pan and continue roasting the chicken until a thermometer inserted into the inner thigh reaches 165°F, 35 to 45 minutes longer.

6 Insert tongs into the cavity of the chicken and press on the lemon halves. Tip the chicken to release any juices into the pan. Transfer the chicken to a carving board and let rest 10 to 15 minutes. Remove and reserve the garlic cloves and discard any herb sprigs from the pan. Using a slotted spoon, transfer the potatoes and onions to a platter and cover with foil to keep warm.

7. Squeeze the garlic cloves from the skins and mash into the juices in the pan. Strain the juices into a pitcher or measuring cup and skim off any excess fat. Season with salt and pepper.

8. Carve the chicken and place on the platter with the potatoes and onions. Serve with the juices alongside in a gravy boat.

TURKEY CHILI

Serves 8

2 cups corn kernels, fresh (from
2 to 3 ears) or frozen, thawed

4 cups low-sodium chicken broth

3 turkey tenderloins (about 2 pounds)

4 tablespoons unsalted butter

1 medium yellow onion, finely chopped

3 celery ribs, finely chopped

2 medium Anaheim chiles or other large
mild chile, seeded and finely chopped

1 medium red bell pepper,
finely chopped

2 garlic cloves, minced

Kosher salt and freshly ground
black pepper

¼ cup fine cornmeal or corn flour

1 tablespoon light brown sugar

2 tablespoons ground cumin

1½ tablespoons ground coriander

1 tablespoon ancho chile powder

2 teaspoons dried oregano

1 (14-ounce) can black beans, drained
and rinsed

For the toppings (optional)

Grated cheddar cheese

Diced red or white onion

Sour cream

Cilantro

This turkey chili is inspired by the best turkey chili we've ever eaten, on a ski mountain in Deer Valley, Utah. It's hearty, delicious, and makes for a perfect winter meal.

1.   In a blender or food processor, puree 1 cup of the corn with ½ cup of the broth.

2.   Chop the turkey into bite-size pieces, removing the tendon as you go.

3.   In a large pot, melt the butter over medium heat. Add the onion, celery, chiles, bell pepper, and garlic. Season with a large pinch of salt and a few grinds of black pepper. Cook, stirring occasionally, until the vegetables are softened, about 8 minutes. Stir in the cornmeal, brown sugar, cumin, coriander, ancho powder, and oregano and cook until fragrant, about 30 seconds.

4.   Add the remaining 3½ cups broth, increase the heat to high, and bring to a boil. Reduce the heat to medium. Add the turkey, corn puree, and black beans and simmer until the turkey is cooked through and the liquid is thickened, about 20 minutes. Add the remaining 1 cup whole corn kernels and heat through. Season with salt and black pepper.

5.   Ladle the chili into bowls, garnish with toppings if desired, and serve.

CHICKEN DRUMSTICK CACCIATORE

Serves 4

3 tablespoons extra-virgin olive oil

10 small chicken drumsticks

1 medium onion, finely chopped

1 medium carrot, chopped

1 medium bulb fennel, quartered, cored, and chopped

8 ounces cremini mushrooms, thinly sliced

2 large garlic cloves, thinly sliced

½ cup dry white or red wine

1 (28-ounce) can tomato puree

1 sprig rosemary

1 (8-ounce) bunch of kale, tough stems and ribs removed, leaves chopped

½ cup chopped sweet pickled peppers

Chopped flat-leaf parsley, for garnish

Another thing we can thank our mom for . . . her penchant for chicken in tomato sauce. This is a really nice dish in colder weather; it's hearty and pairs beautifully with our Cauliflower Couscous (page 181) and a bottle of red.

1. In a large Dutch oven or enameled cast-iron casserole, heat the olive oil over medium-high heat until shimmering. Add half the chicken drumsticks and cook, turning occasionally, until well browned all over, 6 to 8 minutes. Transfer to a plate and repeat with the remaining chicken.

2. Add the onion, carrot, fennel, mushrooms, and garlic to the pot and reduce the heat to medium. Cook, stirring occasionally, until the onion is translucent, about 8 minutes. Add the wine, bring to a boil, and cook until the liquid is evaporated, about 2 minutes. Add the tomato puree and rosemary and return to a boil. Reduce the heat to medium-low and nestle the chicken into the sauce.

3. Cover the pot and simmer for 20 minutes. Add the kale to the top of the stew, cover, and cook until the kale is wilted, about 5 minutes. Stir the kale into the stew and continue cooking until the chicken is very tender, about 20 minutes longer. Stir in the pickled peppers, garnish with parsley, and serve.

WILL SMITH MEETS THE
WOMAN IN WHITE

Danielle's bachelorette celebration consisted of us going by ourselves to the best burlesque show, Le Crazy Horse de Paris, during Paris Fashion Week and a private, intimate dinner with just a few friends at Barbuto when we got back to New York. We chose a quiet four-hour meal over a penis-shaped cake sourced from a special bakery in Chelsea. No male strippers or pink streamers here—just not our style.

A few months later, it was Danielle's new sister-in-law Perry's turn to get married, and both of us were invited to the bachelorette. We were excited for this one, as it would basically

HOUSE OF CARDS RIBS

Serves 6 to 8

For the ribs

2 tablespoons kosher salt

1 tablespoon ground coriander

1 teaspoon smoked paprika

1 teaspoon hot paprika

½ teaspoon freshly ground black pepper

2 racks meaty baby back ribs
(about 6 pounds total)

For the barbecue sauce

2 tablespoons canola oil

1 medium onion, finely chopped

3 garlic cloves, minced

¾ cup ketchup

2 tablespoons bourbon

¼ cup peach jam

2 tablespoons pepper jelly

½ cup apple cider vinegar

2 tablespoons Worcestershire sauce

Kosher salt

Crushed red pepper (optional)

MAKE AHEAD: *The barbecue sauce can be refrigerated for up to 5 days. The baked ribs can be wrapped and refrigerated for up to 3 days before grilling.*

Ribs have always been Laura's specialty. Now, after Frank Underwood from *House of Cards* made us crave ribs basically every day, we call them Laura's "House of Cards Ribs."

1. **PREPARE THE RIBS:** Preheat the oven to 350°F.

2. In a small bowl, mix together the salt, coriander, smoked paprika, hot paprika, and black pepper. Rub the ribs all over with the spice mixture and wrap each rack in a double layer of foil. Arrange the ribs on two baking sheets and bake, rotating the sheets front to back once halfway through, until very tender, about 2 hours.

3. Let the ribs cool slightly and carefully unwrap. Pour the accumulated juices into a large measuring cup and reserve 1 cup for the barbecue sauce. Let the ribs cool completely.

4. **MAKE THE BARBECUE SAUCE:** While the ribs cool, heat the oil in a medium saucepan over medium heat until warmed. Add the onion and cook until softened, about 5 minutes. Add the garlic, and cook until fragrant, 1 to 2 minutes. Add the ketchup, bourbon, peach jam, pepper jelly, vinegar, Worcestershire sauce, and 1 cup reserved meat juices, and bring to a boil over high heat. Reduce the heat to medium-low and simmer until the sauce is thickened and glossy and the flavors have melded, about 20 minutes. Season with salt if needed and crushed red pepper to taste, if desired. (The sauce might taste very vinegary, but it will mellow out on the meat.)

5. Preheat a grill or grill pan over medium-high heat. Grill the ribs, brushing with the sauce and turning frequently, until hot throughout and nicely glazed, about 10 minutes. Transfer the ribs to a carving board and cut between the bones. Serve with the remaining sauce on the side.

QUICK MOROCCAN BEEF STEW WITH PRUNES AND CHICKPEAS

Serves 4

4 tablespoons extra-virgin olive oil

1½ pounds beef tenderloin (filet mignon) or sirloin, cut into 1-inch cubes

Kosher salt and freshly ground black pepper

1 medium onion, finely chopped

2 medium carrots, sliced crosswise on the diagonal, ¼ inch thick

1 tablespoon minced garlic

1 teaspoon ground ginger

1 teaspoon sweet paprika

1 teaspoon ground coriander

½ teaspoon ground cumin

¼ teaspoon ground cinnamon

Pinch of cayenne pepper

2 cups low-sodium beef broth or water

½ cup pitted green olives, thinly sliced

½ cup pitted prunes, chopped

1 (15-ounce) can chickpeas, drained and rinsed

1 lemon

Chopped cilantro or mint, for garnish

Cauliflower Couscous (page 181), for serving

This is one of the only red meat dishes we often make during the week, because it's quick, easy, and healthy. The key to a fast weeknight stew is to start with an already tender cut, like tenderloin. The prunes here thicken the sauce and tame the spices.

1. In a large Dutch oven or enameled cast-iron casserole, heat 2 tablespoons of the oil over medium-high heat until shimmering. Season the beef with salt and black pepper. Working in batches, add a single layer of beef to the pan without the pieces touching and cook, turning, until the pieces are browned, about 5 minutes. Transfer to a clean plate and repeat with the remaining beef.

2. Add the remaining 2 tablespoons oil to the pan and heat over medium heat until warmed. Add the onion and carrots and cook, stirring frequently, until the vegetables are softened, about 8 minutes. Add the garlic and cook until softened, about 2 minutes. Add the spices and cook, stirring, for 30 seconds. Add the broth, olives, prunes, and chickpeas and bring to a boil. Cook until the juices thicken, about 5 minutes.

3. Using a vegetable peeler, remove 1 strip of lemon zest and add it to the pan. Add back the beef and any accumulated juices. Halve the lemon and squeeze the juice from one half into the pan and taste. Add more lemon juice as desired and season with salt and black pepper. Garnish with cilantro or mint and serve with cauliflower couscous.

SOY SAUCE–RUBBED GRILLED STEAK WITH TOMATOES

Serves 4

1 large garlic clove, minced

6 teaspoons reduced-sodium soy sauce

1½ pounds skirt steak, cut crosswise into 4 pieces

2 pounds tomatoes, sliced

2 teaspoons rice vinegar

Freshly ground pepper

1 scallion, thinly sliced

Flaky salt, for serving

This is our go-to dish when we're grilling in the summer and just want to keep it simple. If you can snag some heirloom tomatoes when they're in season, they'll make all the difference.

1. In a small bowl, combine the garlic and 4 teaspoons of the soy sauce. Rub all over the steak and let stand 10 minutes.

2. Preheat a grill or grill pan over medium-high heat.

3. Arrange the tomatoes on a large platter and drizzle with the vinegar and remaining 2 teaspoons soy sauce.

4. Season the steak with pepper, then grill, turning once, until browned on the outside and cooked to medium-rare within, about 4 minutes per side.

5. Arrange the cooked steaks on top of the tomatoes and let rest for 3 minutes. Scatter the sliced scallion around and add a pinch or two of flaky salt on top. Serve.

CHEESEBURGER WITH EASIEST FRIED ONIONS

Serves 4

For the onions

Neutral oil, for frying

2 medium red onions, halved and thinly sliced

Kosher salt

For the burgers

1½ pounds ground beef, preferably 80% lean

Kosher salt and freshly ground pepper

Oil, for the pan

8 slices cheddar cheese

4 potato buns, split and toasted

One summer, we made it our business to try every "best cheeseburger" in New York City, and honestly, we still can't pick a favorite. One of our tops, though, is the burger at the Spotted Pig. Our version pays homage with the quick fried onions, which absolutely make the dish. For the best flavor, buy the best-quality meat you can find and look for meat that's fairly fatty, about 80 percent lean.

1. **PREPARE THE ONIONS:** In a medium saucepan, heat ½ inch neutral oil over medium-high heat. When it's hot enough that it bubbles briskly when a piece of onion is added, carefully add half the onions and fry, stirring occasionally, until browned and crisp, about 9 minutes. (Reduce the heat as needed to prevent the oil from smoking.) Using a slotted spoon, transfer the onions to a plate lined with paper towels to drain. Season generously with salt. Repeat with the remaining onions.

2. **MAKE THE BURGERS:** With your hands, form the ground meat into 4-inch patties about ¾ inch thick, and season generously with salt and lightly with pepper.

3. Heat a cast-iron or other heavy skillet over medium heat until very hot. Use a paper towel to lightly wipe with oil. Add the burgers and cook (working in batches if necessary) until well browned on the bottom, about 5 minutes. Flip and cook to your liking, about 5 minutes longer for medium-rare and 7 minutes for medium. Two minutes before the burgers are done, top each with 2 slices of cheddar. Cover the skillet and let the cheese melt for the last 2 minutes. Transfer the burgers to a plate and let rest for 2 to 3 minutes.

4. Fill the toasted buns with the burgers and onions, then serve.

WHAT TH
"THE NEW

E HELL IS
POTATO"?

*Why did you decide on the name The New Potato?
At this point it's a question we get asked more
than our names. When we came up with the idea for
the website, all we knew was we wanted it to be "The
New . . . Something." It wasn't much to go on.*

When somehow the phrase *The New Potato* came out during a brainstorm over coffee, we liked that it was both a play on *the new black* (as potatoes are a base staple in the world of food, just as the color black is in fashion), and that new potatoes are also an ingredient themselves. We liked that double meaning and decided to go with it.

At first, our relationship with our website name was a little like Ross and Rachel's on *Friends*. We were on-again, off-again. Some days we loved each other, some days we hated each other, but in the end we were meant to end up together. Everyone else saw it, so why couldn't we?

It took us a while to realize our brand name set us apart from other online magazines. The exact qualities that made us nervous about it were the very things people loved most about it. Its playfulness made us worry it wouldn't be taken seriously. Its shabby chic nature made us worry it wouldn't be highbrow enough. The infinite number of possible puns and spinoffs it allowed for would sometimes annoy us. And its originality made it a constant conversation piece, taking up valuable time that should have been spent talking about the brand mission.

But the thing we always loved about The New Potato—especially in the beginning—was that people didn't forget it.

In a brave new world where millions of websites spring up each day and content is king, it helped us that people walked away from initial conversations chuckling about "the potato girls," as we've come to be called by many. Whether they knew what the brand was or didn't (yet), they didn't forget the name, and sometimes that's all it takes at first.

Sure, there were times we wished we were called something more serious—our first Paris Fashion Week when we almost got detained at customs by a French government official who hadn't heard of a magazine called "Zee New Potato."

"What does zis mean?" he asked skeptically.

We did our Two-Man Show.

"Well, it's like the new black in fashion. . . ."

Jazz hands, jazz hands.

"Only in food, because potatoes are the most basic of ingredients, the black of fashion if you will. . . ."

Tap, tap, tap.

"Plus new potatoes are an actual ingredient, so it has a double meaning."

Jazz hands, jazz hands, jazz hands.

He called for backup. Just kidding, but it was only one of many instances when we wished we'd opted for something of a more "serious" persuasion.

There was also always the dreaded question: "So, do you guys just really like potatoes?" The first to ask was Giuliana Rancic during her interview, and it took more than one try to explain that nothing had anything to do with actual potatoes. The same happened with many celebrities we'd interview in the first few months. They'd come from meetings with the *New York Times, Vanity Fair,* and *People,* to be interviewed by The New Potato—a new "hit publication" their publicist hadn't had time to explain to them.

"But I don't eat potatoes really," one actress shot off.

"She's actually on a juice cleanse this month," a rep wrote in reply to a pitch.

After six months of jazz hands and tap dancing, we were invited to sit front row at Christian Siriano's fashion show. Considering how briefly we'd been around, we were honored, and couldn't believe when our friend, who'd done the styling for the show, told us Christian (now our friend) was excited we were there.

BUT THE THING WE ALWAYS LOVED ABOUT THE NEW POTATO— ESPECIALLY IN THE BEGINNING—WAS THAT PEOPLE DIDN'T FORGET IT.

"He really was excited?" Danielle asked.

"Yes!" she told us. "He came backstage after the show and said, 'The potatoes came!'"

We weren't totally positive what to make of our new title, but we figured Mary-Kate and Ashley Olsen were the Row; Kourtney, Kim, and Khloé were the Kardashians; and we were the Potatoes. Sometimes we were the Potato Girls, sometimes Potato 1 & 2, sometimes the Hot Potatoes, sometimes the Mashed Potatoes, and heck, when Katie Couric met our parents she said, "So you're the old potatoes!"

Not only did we embrace our brand, but we also embraced new potatoes as a food. It's no secret they make for a delicious side dish. But just like our website isn't all about spuds, this sides chapter isn't all about them either. When it comes to new and inventive side dishes, we always keep our eyes peeled. Get it?

ROSEMARY NEW POTATOES

Serves 4 to 6

This was one of our favorite things our mom made when we were growing up. We liked when she roasted the potatoes to almost potato chip level, even slightly burned them, but you can cook to your preference.

1½ pounds baby potatoes, thinly sliced
2 tablespoons extra-virgin olive oil
1 tablespoon chopped rosemary
Kosher salt and freshly ground pepper

1. Preheat the oven to 400°F.

2. In a large bowl, toss the potatoes with the olive oil and rosemary and season with salt and pepper.

3. Spread them out on a baking sheet so they're in a single layer. (Use two baking sheets if necessary.) Roast until the potatoes are nicely browned on the bottom, with some getting totally crisp, like potato chips, and others staying a bit tender within, 15 to 20 minutes.

4. Let cool on the baking sheet, then transfer to a bowl and serve.

NEW POTATO SALAD WITH RADISHES, FENNEL, AND CELERY

Serves 4

1 pound baby potatoes

2 tablespoons apple cider vinegar or white wine vinegar

1 teaspoon Dijon mustard

3 tablespoons sunflower or safflower oil

4 medium red radishes, halved and thinly sliced (about 1 cup)

3 medium celery ribs, thinly sliced crosswise on the diagonal (about ½ cup)

1 small fennel bulb, halved, cored, and cut into bite-size pieces

Kosher salt and freshly ground pepper

2 tablespoons chopped dill

Best served with our Easy Veal Schnitzel (page 151), but also delicious as a side for summer BBQs. The crunchiness of the radish, fennel, and celery is lovely against the soft potatoes.

1. In a large pot, cover the potatoes with water and bring to a boil over high heat. Reduce the heat to medium and simmer until tender, about 15 minutes. Drain and let cool.

2. In a large bowl, whisk together the vinegar, mustard, and oil. Add the radishes, celery, and fennel. Slice the potatoes into rounds (removing the peel if you prefer) and add to the bowl. Stir together and season the salad with salt and pepper. Fold in the dill. Serve immediately or refrigerate for up to 1 day.

LEMON-DILL MASHED POTATO CAKES

Makes 8 cakes

2 pounds potatoes, such as Idaho or Yukon Gold, peeled and cut into 1- to 2-inch pieces

2½ teaspoons kosher salt

¼ cup grated onion

1 egg, lightly beaten

¼ cup whole-milk or 2% Greek yogurt

3 tablespoons all-purpose flour

¼ cup finely chopped dill

Grated zest of 1 lemon

Freshly ground pepper

1 tablespoon unsalted butter

2 tablespoons neutral oil

These mashed potato cakes are perfect when we want something a little more exciting than veggies—or for breakfast as part of our Eggs Benedict recipe (page 36)!

1.   In a large saucepan, cover the potatoes with water and add 1 teaspoon of the salt. Bring to a boil over high heat and cook until the potatoes are tender, about 20 minutes. Drain and return the potatoes to the pan. Cook over medium heat until dry, about 1 minute. Mash the potatoes and let cool to room temperature or refrigerate overnight.

2.   Add the onion, egg, yogurt, flour, dill, lemon zest, pepper to taste, and the remaining 1½ teaspoons salt to the mashed potatoes. Stir until incorporated, adding a little more flour if the mixture seems wet or a little more yogurt if the mixture seems dry.

3.   In a large skillet, melt the butter in the oil over medium-high heat. Scoop 4 heaping ⅓ cups of the mixture into the skillet and cook until the cakes are fragrant, about 2 minutes. Reduce the heat to low and cook until the bottoms are a deep golden brown, about 4 minutes. Increase the heat to medium-high, flip the cakes, and cook for 2 minutes followed by another 4 minutes on medium-low heat. Transfer to a plate lined with paper towels to drain. Repeat with the remaining mixture, adding more oil if necessary, to make 8 cakes total.

4.   Serve hot or warm.

CAULIFLOWER COUSCOUS

Makes about 4 cups

1 medium head cauliflower (about
2 pounds) or 1 pound riced cauliflower

2 tablespoons extra-virgin olive oil

Kosher salt and freshly ground pepper

This is a great healthy alternative to rice or pasta. It soaks up the juices from a dish the way rice would, and pairs well with just about anything.

1.   Halve the cauliflower and pull off all the leaves. Remove the tough core and break the cauliflower into large florets. Put half of the florets in a food processor and pulse until it looks like couscous. Transfer to a bowl and repeat with the remaining cauliflower.

2.   In a large, heavy saucepan, heat the olive oil over medium heat. Add the cauliflower and a large pinch of salt and stir to coat with the fat. Cover and cook, stirring once or twice, until tender, about 8 minutes. Season with salt and pepper and serve.

CRISP BOK CHOY WITH MISO

Serves 4

1 tablespoon white miso

1 tablespoon rice vinegar

½ teaspoon sugar

2 tablespoons neutral oil

1 pound bok choy, sliced crosswise,
stems and leaves kept separate

Kosher salt

2 garlic cloves, minced

2 scallions, thinly sliced

1.   In a small bowl, whisk together the miso, vinegar, and sugar.

2.   In a large deep skillet or wok, heat 1 tablespoon of the oil over high heat until shimmering. Add the bok choy stems and a small pinch of salt and cook, stirring constantly, until starting to soften, about 3 minutes. Add the leaves and cook, stirring constantly, until wilted and the stems are crisp-tender, about 2 minutes longer. Add the remaining 1 tablespoon oil and the garlic and scallions and cook, stirring constantly, until fragrant, about 1 minute. Remove the pan from the heat and stir in the miso sauce. Season with more salt, if needed, then serve.

GRILLED EGGPLANT AND ZUCCHINI WITH SMOKED ALMOND–CILANTRO PESTO

Serves 4 to 6

3 cups cilantro leaves and tender stems

1 cup smoked or roasted almonds

1 medium garlic clove

2 tablespoons sherry vinegar or aged white wine vinegar

¾ cup extra-virgin olive oil, plus more for brushing

Kosher salt

1 pound eggplant (2 medium), thinly sliced lengthwise

1 pound zucchini (2 large), halved crosswise and thinly sliced lengthwise

Freshly ground pepper

MAKE AHEAD: *The pesto can be refrigerated in an airtight container for up to 5 days or frozen for up to 2 months.*

This pesto is vegan and contains a lot of nuts, which makes the dish a substantial side. It's really nice with a piece of fish. You could also chop the vegetables and toss them, along with the pesto, with pasta for an easy weeknight meal.

1.   In a food processor, pulse together the cilantro, almonds, and garlic until finely chopped. With the machine running, add the vinegar and ¾ cup olive oil until coarsely pureed. Season with salt.

2.   Preheat a grill or grill pan to medium-high heat. Brush the eggplant and zucchini with olive oil and season with salt and pepper. Grill until marks appear and the vegetables are tender, turning once, about 4 minutes per side. Arrange the vegetables on a platter and dollop with some of the pesto, passing more at the table.

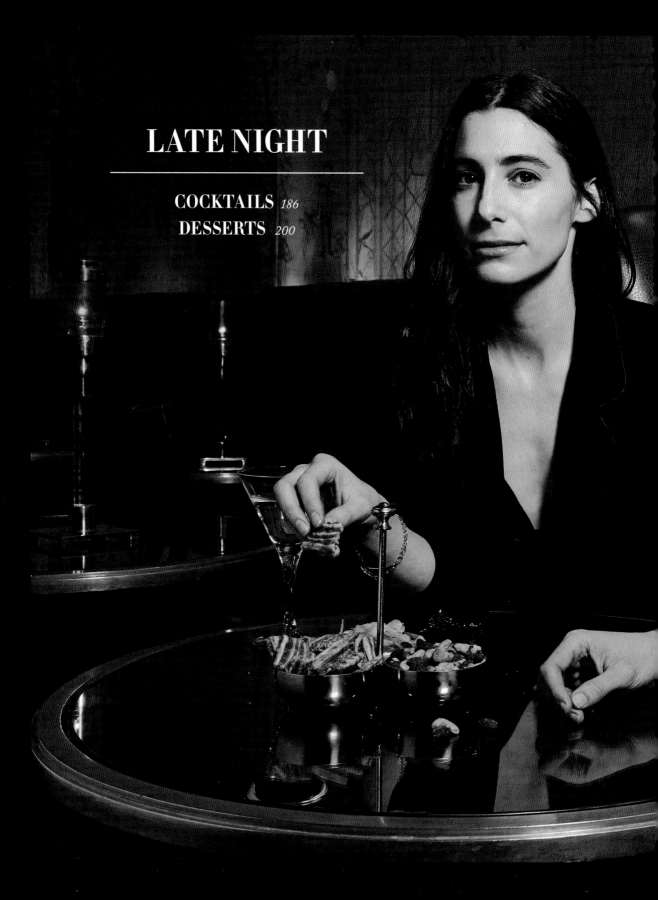

LATE NIGHT

THE TIME WE MADE BETHENNY FRANKEL'S SHIT LIST

(OR DID WE?)

W hen we were asked to be media sponsors at the
New York City Wine & Food Festival, we were
convinced it was our big break. Not only had we been
approached to collaborate on one of the events, but that
collaboration took the form of cohosting a two–hundred–
person Cocktails Ever After soirée at the Dream
Downtown hotel with none other than Skinnygirl
Bethenny Frankel.

Cohosting is a loose term. It turns out there are big breaks and then there are fake big breaks. Big breaks can make a career; fake ones are something you look back on with the same whimsy you reserve for a goofy childhood photo. This event would no doubt go down in history as our large fake big break . . . meaning it wouldn't go down in history at all.

The fact that we had *one* assignment only—to make cocktail cards presenting a contest for a Skinnygirl gift pack—should have been our first tip-off. It's like cohosting a humongous party with someone and being in charge of cups and ice.

As you may or may not know, Bethenny's Skinnygirl Cocktails are the embodiment of the maxim Drink like a lady. So for the cards we thought we'd have guests answer the question "How do you drink like a lady?" and fill in the blank in this sentence: **"A Lady Always _____ While Cocktailing,"** adding their email addresses at the bottom. We'd pick the winner, post on The New Potato, and they'd win the aforementioned Skinnygirl gift pack.

In typical Danielle fashion, she slaved over the cards for months. Fonts, colors, and logos became her obsession, and the PDF draft of the card passed through the Kosann family for approval like wildfire. Questions shot back and forth:

"Is the red *too* red?"

"No. But is the black too black?"

"I don't think black can be too black. But the white almost seems too white?"

"Does a girl holding a cocktail *actually* look like that?"

"What else would she look like? But feel free to send another option. . . ."

Every possible query was addressed, every discrepancy that existed was combed over, until we had the most perfect cocktail card on this side of the Atlantic. Or so we thought.

The big night arrived. We expected to be Bethenny's BFFs by the end of the evening—we were cohosts after all, practically confidantes.

"Maybe we'll do drinks with Bethenny after the party?" Danielle asked casually as we got out of the cab.

"Oh, totally," Laura said, as if she was answering the question "Is the world round?"

There'd be around two hundred guests, but we'd printed a thousand cards so there was *no possible way* anyone would miss them. Even though we planned to hand them out as people walked in, we also got there early to distribute and stack them on every table and in every corner and crevice of the room. These cards basically replaced the tiling. Each card had The New Potato logo right at the top; you couldn't miss it—this was branding at its absolute finest.

Two of our friends came to help us that night, and five minutes before the guests were let in, we gave Nikki stacks to have at the ready and asked Danielle's friend Rory to go check out the line outside. Nikki looked down at her stack and immediately looked back up.

"Um . . . guys?" Nikki said.

"What's up?" Laura asked.

WE LOOKED DOWN. AND THERE IT WAS, SMACK IN THE MIDDLE, THE STAR OF THE SHOW.

"They're great, right?" Danielle glowed. The cards were her Sistine Chapel.

"Well, there's a typo."

We looked at each other, telepathically coming to the conclusion that this girl couldn't possibly spell. We—as well as the rest of the Kosann family—had reviewed this card, analyzed this card, loved this card . . . a typo was an impossibility.

We looked down. And there it was, smack in the middle, the star of the show:

A Lady Alway __ While Cocktailing

Oh my god.

"We're about to let the guests in!" the press rep yelled to us from the doorway.

Have you ever met fans of Bethenny Frankel? This wasn't a slow stream of people trickling in for casual cocktails and appetizers; this was more like a Justin Bieber concert. People waited outside, two hundred of them, ready to rush in, grab their cocktail cards, and wait for the Skinnygirl herself. Sure, we could hold off on handing the cards out, but we had seen to it that every square foot of the room was covered in cards. There was no iCloud we could make an edit on; there were a thousand printed cards missing a thousand S's.

So this is why they say print is dead, we thought. We looked at each other.

Danielle's head tilted: *We could make a run for it?*

Laura squinted: *To where? Canada?*

Danielle slightly shrugged: *Maybe no one will notice.*

"Guys, did you know this says 'alway' not 'always'?" Rory, who had just come back in, asked. "Was that on purpose?"

Yes, Rory, that was on purpose.

The guests started to pour in and we knew we had only one choice: Start drinking heavily.

We passed out the cards in a halfhearted kind of way, murmuring the instructions to guests, then scampering away before a tipsy girl in heels would say something like "It's alwayS, not alway!"

To add insult to injury, we never even met Bethenny. She got escorted in and sat in a roped VIP area while guests waited in line to take photos with her. We're not even sure she knew she had "cohosts" or cocktail cards, but at that point we'd been so panicked she'd be pissed about the typo that we were more than happy to pass into nonexistence.

If you thought something like "A Lady Alway *Uses an S* While Cocktailing" was an original joke in this situation, let us tell you, it wasn't. Around two hundred cards said that, and if they didn't say that, they had a capital *S* circled five times after "Alway." The letter *S* has haunted us ever since.

Do you need a good cocktail after reading that anxiety-filled story? Well, you're in luck.

GRAPEFRUIT MARGARITA

Makes 1 drink

Ice

3 tablespoons fresh grapefruit juice

3 tablespoons tequila

1 tablespoon fresh lime juice

2 teaspoons simple syrup (see Note)
or honey

In an ice-filled shaker, combine the
grapefruit juice, tequila, lime juice,
and simple syrup and shake well.
Strain into an ice-filled rocks glass.

NOTE: *To make simple syrup, combine
2 teaspoons sugar with 2 teaspoons
water and heat in a microwave for 15 to
30 seconds, until the sugar is dissolved.
Refrigerate until chilled. Alternatively, do
this on a stovetop.*

MOSCOW MULE

Makes 1 drink

Ice
¼ cup vodka
½ cup ginger beer
Juice of ½ lime
Lime wheel, for garnish

Fill a Collins glass or copper mug with ice. Add the vodka, ginger beer, and lime juice and stir. Garnish with a lime wheel.

OUR (VERY DRY) VODKA MARTINI

Makes 1 drink

Ice
¼ cup plus 2 tablespoons vodka
1 tablespoon dry vermouth
Large green olives, for serving

In an ice-filled mixing glass, combine the vodka and vermouth. Stir until well chilled, then strain into a martini glass. Add olives to the glass and serve.

NOTE: *If you're like Laura, and mostly just like the vodka, don't even add the vermouth in the cocktail. Just put it in the martini glass, turn the glass to coat the sides, and dump it out. Then make the martini with vodka and ice.*

WHEN DANIELLE PHOTOGRAPHED THE ACTOR PEDRO PASCAL FOR THE NEW POTATO, IT WAS TRULY HIS MOMENT. HE HAD BEEN A FAN FAVORITE CHARACTER, OBERYN, ON *GAME OF THRONES*, WHO, SPOILER ALERT, HAD JUST BEEN KILLED OFF IN SPECTACULAR FASHION. HE WAS ALSO SOON TO STAR IN NETFLIX'S SOON-TO-BE HIT SERIES *NARCOS*.

"IT'S COMPLICATED" WITH THAT HUNK ON GAME OF THRONES

Being just the two of us working on the site, sometimes we had to delegate, and shooting a super-hot guy we both had a crush on was no exception. Laura was having serious FOMO about missing this one.

Danielle was to photograph Pedro in Central Park, as he was in *Much Ado About Nothing* at Shakespeare in the Park that summer. It was a very hot day (all puns intended) and a restaurant—the Smith—was the backup plan, since there was a chance of rain. Laura reluctantly stayed behind to do computer work but instructed Danielle to call her the minute she was done.

As fate would have it, the rain started coming down as both Danielle and Pedro made their way to the meeting spot in the park. *I know I just got married,* Danielle thought, *but could this be any more like* The Notebook? She kept the notion to herself rather than text it to Laura.

Danielle approached Pedro like a schoolgirl, giggling and apologizing about the rain and suggesting the alternative: "I'll do whatever you like, if you want to, you know, we can just, do that."

"That sounds great," Pedro said.

While Laura—the writer—would have been ashamed of Danielle's inability to complete a sentence, Danielle smiled to herself: *Looks like I've still got it.*

They headed to the Smith as the rain poured down. It wasn't a short walk.

"So how was it?" Laura's text read thirty-five minutes later.

"Still together," Danielle quickly wrote back.

Laura responded, "What does that mean?"

No answer.

As the two walked side by side in the rain, Danielle couldn't help but notice the looks they were getting. They got stopped twice by fans and—as she had ditched her usual casual photography outfit for a far cuter summer dress—she was pretty sure they were getting mistaken for Dedro. What's Dedro, you ask? Danielle + Pedro . . . the celebrity name Danielle had thought up around the time they passed 78th Street. Duh.

Dedro has such a ring to it, Danielle mused. She then thought about what her and her husband Seth's celebrity name combo would be: Deth. *Yikes. How is this the first time I've thought about that?* But she brushed the thought aside as they reached the restaurant.

"Mind if I take my shirt off?" Pedro asked.

They had just arrived at the private room at the Smith.

"Um . . . sorry?"

"It's just it's soaking wet. Do you mind?" he said as he started pulling it off.

Danielle attempted nonchalance with every fiber of her being. "Sure."

"Did you finish yet?" Laura's newest text read.

"He just took his shirt off," Danielle wrote back. And yes, that's all Danielle wrote back.

Danielle could hear Laura's head exploding somewhere, Danielle's head was exploding, and of course this is all ironic because Oberyn died in *Game of Thrones* from—well—his head exploding. This all seemed fated.

"So where do you want me?" Pedro asked.

Sorry, guys, we promise this story doesn't turn into a porno.

"Actually," he continued, "can we wait for my shirt to dry? That's the one I'd wanted to wear for this, not this one." He had changed into a T-shirt he had in his bag.

"Of course!" Danielle said.

"I'm going to grab a beer, do you want anything?" Pedro asked.

If there was ever a time to drink on the job, it was now.

"Sure, a Chardonnay would be great."

Pedro went to get the drinks, Danielle took deep breaths, and Laura sat in her apartment convinced there was some sort of *Fifty Shades of Grey* + *Game of Thrones* situation happening at the Smith right now.

"He took his shirt off to dry, we're having a drink while we wait," Danielle texted back to Laura's sea of exclamation points, question marks, and emojis.

As Danielle and Pedro sat and chatted, she tried not to keel over, as, like any good actor, he didn't break eye contact.

"So, you're married?" Pedro said at some point, pointing to her engagement ring.

Danielle was slightly tempted to come out with something like "Oh, what, this old thing?"

Instead she told the truth, his shirt eventually dried, and the shoot was a success. Whether it is with Brad Pitt or Betty White, Laura now insists on making her *own* decisions when it comes to missing photo shoots.

***

Yep, that actually happened. Even if Pedro won't be there to join you, we're pretty sure a good cocktail will make any rainy day better. Or any day at all, for that matter.

BOURBON CHAI

Makes 1 drink

½ cup whole milk or full-fat coconut milk

1 teaspoon loose black tea or 1 English breakfast tea bag

1 teaspoon light brown sugar, or more to taste

4 black peppercorns

2 thin slices fresh ginger

2 green cardamom pods, crushed

¼ teaspoon fennel seeds

2 whole cloves

1 tablespoon bourbon, or more to taste

There is nothing better than a chai latte in winter—except a chai latte with bourbon.

1. In a small saucepan, combine the milk and ¾ cup water and bring to a simmer over medium heat. Add the tea, brown sugar, and spices and simmer for 1 minute. Remove the pan from the heat and let the tea stand until the flavor is infused, about 10 minutes. Strain the chai through a fine-mesh sieve into a liquid measuring cup. Pour back into the saucepan and reheat over medium heat.

2. Pour the bourbon into a mug and top with the tea. Add more sugar and bourbon, if desired, and serve.

ROASTED TOMATO BLOODY MARY

Makes 4 drinks

2 pounds tomatoes, halved

Extra-virgin olive oil, for rubbing

3 tablespoons fresh lemon juice

1½ tablespoons Worcestershire sauce

1 teaspoon prepared horseradish

½ teaspoon Old Bay seasoning,
plus more to taste

1 teaspoon kosher salt, plus more to taste

Sugar (optional)

½ cup vodka

Celery ribs, olives, and lemon wedges,
for garnish

MAKE AHEAD: *The Bloody Mary mix can be refrigerated in a glass jar for up to 5 days.*

Everyone should have a Bloody Mary in his or her repertoire. The roasted tomato really elevates this one and deepens the flavor.

1. Preheat the oven to 400°F. Line a baking sheet with parchment paper.

2. Rub the tomatoes on all sides with olive oil and arrange them cut side down on the prepared baking sheet. Roast until very soft and the skins are shriveled, 30 to 40 minutes. Let the tomatoes cool slightly, then pinch off the skins. Transfer the tomatoes and any accumulated juices to a blender or food processor and puree until smooth.

3. Strain the tomato juice through a fine-mesh sieve into a pitcher or liquid measuring cup. Add the lemon juice, Worcestershire sauce, horseradish, Old Bay, and salt. Taste and add more salt or Old Bay or a pinch of sugar if needed.

4. Chill the mix for at least 1 hour.

5. For each drink, combine ½ cup mix with 2 tablespoons vodka in ice-filled Collins glasses. Garnish with celery ribs, olives, and lemon wedges and serve.

MARTHA STEWART

AS ALWAYS PERFEC

*W*e were attending a demo that was in celebration of Martha's then-latest book, Martha Stewart's Cakes, *and with the new release we'd scored our first big interview, a quick chat with Martha afterward. It was the quintessential get for a food website: a talk with the queen of all things style, home, and culinary. To say we were scared to death was putting it mildly. What could we possibly ask Martha Stewart that hadn't been asked before?*

We hadn't realized the event where we were meeting her was a formal demo. Everyone seemed to have a master's degree in glazing, and when it came to our tiny New York kitchens, let's just say there was nary a rolling pin in sight.

Danielle arrived on time and snagged seats front row and center. Laura, however, was running late. Very late. The women around Danielle eyed the Bundts, loaves, and layer cakes the way chemists study their test tubes. She tried to emulate their fervor.

Martha's green button-down shirt sat perfectly, as did her blond hair, as did the caramel glaze she was drizzling. Predictably, everything at the front of the room had one common denominator: perfection.

Finally Martha looked up, and without even having to raise a hand or make an announcement, the room went quiet. The empty seat next to Danielle was making her all but perspire onto the coffee cake two feet in front of her. She had no knowledge of Laura's whereabouts because checking your phone in the presence of Martha was sacrilegious. As Martha said something like "Thank you, everyone, for coming," Laura hurried in, looking utterly petrified.

She mouthed something like "such bad traffic" to Danielle, but Danielle pretended not to know her and stared at Martha, ready and eager to share an eye-roll about this latecomer. Danielle was prepared to write off our blood relation completely, but Martha looked past both of us as if we were translucent.

The demo, of course, went smoothly. In fact, the only low point in the demo was Laura's—and it was worse than being late. While using the mixer to beat some eggs, Martha asked, "Does anyone in here not own a stand mixer?" Even Elmer Fudd would have known not to raise his hand, but Laura shot hers up in the air.

Martha eyed the crowd as Laura slowly lowered her hand back down a bit, catching wind of Danielle's sigh and the fact that there was not another hand raised in that room. It was a silence that seemed to resonate through the entirety of New York City. After an awkward pause, Martha said, "Good, no one," and moved on.

After Martha took questions from the crowd—all of which seemed to have been prepared two weeks prior and rehearsed like an Academy Awards acceptance speech—she ducked out, and her PR rep waved to us to follow her down a hallway.

We arrived at an empty conference room and were told to wait for her there. We eyed the chairs at the large table, having no clue what the setup should be for our chat. Should we sit? Should we stand and wait for Martha to arrive to see where she sat? Should we sit, then stand to greet her? We danced and paced and plotted; picked chairs up and moved them side to side, standing and inspecting like interior decorators. Martha might have been proud of our attempts at revamping.

We ended up with the exact setup we had walked into, finally taking a breath and just sitting down, leaving the seat between us open for Martha. Suddenly she whisked in (pun intended), made introductions, and simply leaned against the table, standing above us and waiting for our questions. We stared up at her, then shot up out of our chairs and proceeded to do the interview standing.

It was a success: Martha told us about her new penchant for okra, why she brings fresh eggs for the host/hostess when she goes to parties, and that time Bill and Hillary Clinton came over for cappuccinos. She also gave us a mean recipe for mini rum Bundt cakes that's on our website.

The best part of the interview, though, was Martha's answer to the question "Is there one thing you know now that you wish you'd known when you started?" Without so much as a pause, Martha laughed and said, "Um . . . no."

Can we make desserts like Martha? Absolutely not. But we can certainly try—and ours are pretty damn good.

SWEET-and-SALTY MOLTEN CHOCOLATE CAKES

Makes 4 cakes

1 stick (4 ounces) salted butter

Turbinado sugar (such as Sugar
in the Raw), for dusting

5 ounces bittersweet chocolate,
finely chopped

⅓ cup granulated or organic cane sugar

3 large eggs

¼ cup almond flour

Flaky salt, for sprinkling

This super-delicious, melt-in-your-mouth cake happens to be gluten-free! You'll need ramekins to make this, but they're totally worth the (tiny) investment. After you have them, you'll find you use them for everything: serving olives and nuts, as bowls for your morning yogurt, and to hold prepped ingredients as you cook.

1. Preheat the oven to 425°F. Melt 1 tablespoon of the butter and use it to brush four 6-ounce ramekins. Dust the ramekins with turbinado sugar, tapping out any excess. Transfer to a baking sheet.

2. In a small saucepan, combine the remaining 7 tablespoons butter and the chocolate and cook over medium-low heat, stirring constantly, until the chocolate is melted. Remove the pan from the heat and let the chocolate cool.

3. In a medium bowl, beat the granulated sugar and eggs until pale and frothy, about 3 minutes. Fold in the chocolate mixture, followed by the almond flour. Divide the batter among the prepared ramekins.

4. Bake until the tops are firm but the cakes wobble slightly when jiggled, 11 to 13 minutes. Let them cool for about 1 minute, then run a knife around the edges of the cake and invert onto small plates. Sprinkle each with a pinch of flaky salt and serve immediately.

APPLE STRUDEL

Makes 2 strudels

1 pound Granny Smith apples, peeled
and chopped into bite-size pieces

¼ cup chopped walnuts

¼ cup golden raisins

¼ cup sugar

¼ teaspoon ground cinnamon

Pinch of kosher salt

6 sheets phyllo (from 1 package)

4 tablespoons unsalted butter, melted

¼ cup dried bread crumbs

MAKE AHEAD: *The strudels are best the day they're made but can be wrapped and stored at room temperature for up to 2 days; rewarm in a 300°F oven.*

This is Grandmommy's recipe—one that she's been making for us since we were kids. We tried every variation under the sun to make it our own: healthier, caramelized, different types of nuts . . . but the fact remained, nothing compared to the original. Thanks, Grandmommy!

1. Preheat the oven to 425°F. Line a baking sheet with parchment paper.

2. In a large bowl, toss together the apples, walnuts, raisins, sugar, cinnamon, and salt.

3. Arrange a barely damp towel on a work surface. Set a stack of 3 sheets of phyllo on the towel with the long side facing you, leaving the remaining 3 sheets covered with plastic. Brush the top sheet with butter.

4. Spread half of the bread crumbs along the bottom third of the phyllo about 1 inch in from the bottom edge of the dough, leaving 1 inch on either side of the dough. Top with half the filling. Fold the sides in toward the filling, then roll up the phyllo to encase the filling. Transfer the unbaked strudel to the prepared baking sheet seam side down. Use a sharp knife to cut three or four slits for steam to vent. Brush the top of the strudel with butter.

5. Repeat with the remaining phyllo, bread crumbs, and filling to make the second strudel.

6. Bake the strudels until the tops are golden, about 20 minutes, rotating the pan front to back halfway through. Transfer the baking sheet to a rack and let the strudels cool. Serve slightly warm or at room temperature.

SWEET POTATO CHEESECAKE

Makes one 8-inch cake

1 large sweet potato (about 1 pound)

16 graham crackers (9 ounces)

½ cup walnut halves

¾ cup plus 1 tablespoon sugar

¾ teaspoon kosher salt

1 stick (4 ounces) unsalted
butter, melted

1 pound cream cheese, at
room temperature

1 cup whole-milk Greek yogurt,
at room temperature

¼ cup pure maple syrup

1 teaspoon vanilla extract

3 large eggs, at room temperature

MAKE AHEAD: *The cake can be refrigerated
for up to 3 days. Or it can be frozen: Slice
the cake and freeze the individual slices on a
baking sheet. Once frozen, wrap each slice in
plastic and freeze for up to 2 months. Thaw
in the refrigerator.*

1.   Position a rack in the center of the oven and preheat to 350°F.

2.   Prick the sweet potato all over with a fork and set it in a small baking dish. Bake until cooked through, about 1 hour. Leaving the oven on, remove the potato. Let cool, then peel off the skin and mash the flesh with a fork.

3.   Meanwhile, in a food processor, pulse the graham crackers with the walnuts until finely ground. Add 1 tablespoon of the sugar and ¼ teaspoon of the salt and pulse. Add the melted butter and pulse until incorporated.

4.   Transfer the mixture to an 8-inch springform pan, and using the bottom of a glass, press the crumbs into the bottom and up the sides of the pan. Bake until the edges start to brown, about 12 minutes. Remove from the oven to cool slightly, but leave the oven on and reduce the oven temperature to 300°F.

5.   In a clean food processor, pulse the cream cheese with the remaining ¾ cup sugar until smooth. Add the Greek yogurt, maple syrup, vanilla, and remaining ½ teaspoon salt and puree. Add the eggs, one at a time, and pulse until incorporated. Add the cooled mashed sweet potato and pulse just until combined.

6.   Pour the filling into the cooled crust and transfer the pan to a baking sheet. Bake until the edges are set and the center is a little jiggly, about 1 hour 10 minutes.

7.   Transfer the cake to a rack and let cool for 1 hour. Run a knife around the edge of the cake and then refrigerate until chilled, at least 2 hours and up to overnight before serving.

PEACHES, CREAM, AND SLEEP-AWAY CAMP

A long, long time ago, in a galaxy far, far away
at a Jewish girls summer camp in Maine, we
made our dance debut as sisters to the song "Peaches
& Cream" by the R&B band 112. Always the foodies,
we picked the song based on how nice the dessert these
guys were rapping about sounded, not knowing what
the true meaning of the song was. (This is a cookbook,
so we'll let you look that up on your own time.)

While the only time we *danced* to a song
about "dessert" was at the camp talent show,
the rest of the time at our summer camp also
revolved around our and everyone's sweet tooth.
Candy wasn't allowed, so naturally the stuff was
smuggled in and out any and every way possible.
Parents strapped Swedish Fish to their thighs on
visiting day, brothers from neighboring camps
taped Charleston Chews into the linings of their
backpacks on brothers day, and at nighttime a
bunk-hopping candy-bartering economy thrived
as Jawbreakers were traded for Skittles—and Sour
Patch Watermelon was the equivalent of gold.

Don't get us wrong—we had plenty of "legal"
opportunities to indulge. The cookie line opened at
eleven-fifteen a.m. on the dot each day. Girls would
line up outside the mess hall for their one allotted
cookie—though you could get two or three if you
knew how to trick the kitchen staff (Laura was
particularly good at this in her heyday), and again
camp would become what we imagine happens in
prison when something valuable is traded, consumed,
or confiscated.

Ironically, our Grandmommy always called camp
"the prison," and during the two "grandparent" phone

ROSEMARY SEA SALT SHORTBREAD

Makes about 32 cookies

⅓ cup granulated sugar

2 teaspoons finely chopped rosemary

⅓ cup powdered sugar

2 sticks (8 ounces) unsalted butter, at room temperature

2 cups all-purpose flour

1 teaspoon kosher salt

Flaky salt, for sprinkling

MAKE AHEAD: *The paper-wrapped dough can be wrapped in plastic and frozen for up to 2 months. Thaw slightly before slicing and baking.*

The cookie dough here gets chilled twice (once for at least 45 minutes). The waiting is so worth it because you end up with crisp but tender cookies. We add powdered sugar, too, to make these even crisper. We love the rosemary here, but you could make these with sage, lavender, or dried rose petals instead.

1. In a large bowl, rub the granulated sugar with the chopped rosemary until fragrant. Stir in the powdered sugar. Using a handheld electric mixer, beat in the butter at medium speed. At low speed, beat in the flour and salt until a soft dough forms.

2. Divide the dough in half and transfer to 2 sheets of wax or parchment paper and refrigerate for 20 minutes. Form the dough into two 4-inch logs, wrap in the wax paper, and refrigerate until very firm, about 45 minutes or up to 3 days.

3. Position two racks in the upper and lower thirds of the oven and preheat the oven to 350°F.

4. Cut the chilled shortbread dough into ¼-inch-thick slices and arrange the rounds about 1½ inches apart on two large ungreased baking sheets. Sprinkle with flaky salt, then freeze for 10 minutes.

5. Bake the shortbread until the edges are lightly browned, 15 to 20 minutes, rotating the baking sheets halfway through. Transfer to a wire rack to cool completely.

Thank you to Amanda Englander, our editor, for making this book happen, and to the wonderful team at Clarkson Potter: Doris Cooper, Ian Dingman, Christine Tanigawa, Heather Williamson, Kevin Sweeting, Natasha Martin, and Erin Voigt; and our amazing photographer Aubrie Pick and Cortney Munna. Thank you to our recipe maven Kristin Donnelly; our favorite agent, Margaret Riley King, for always having our back; our associate editor, Catherine Collentine, without whom we could never have found the time to do this book; Laura Brown, Aubrey Anderson Emmons, Katie Couric, and all the other fantastic people who inspired us to write the stories that make this book what it is; Christina Tosi, for your endless support and inspiration; our family and friends, for always being there; our grandmother Katharina Perlow, for making us love food, and our grandfather Bill Perlow, for being one of the best people to share a meal with; Seth and Matt (We love you!); and lastly to our parents, Monica and Rod Kosann, who always told us anything was possible.

Copyright © 2018 by Danielle Kosann and Laura Kosann
Photographs copyright © 2018 by Aubrie Pick

Published in the United States by Clarkson Potter/
Publishers, an imprint of the Crown Publishing Group, a
division of Penguin Random House LLC, New York.
crownpublishing.com
clarksonpotter.com

CLARKSON POTTER is a trademark and POTTER
with colophon is a registered trademark of Penguin Random
House LLC.

Library of Congress Cataloging-in-Publication Data
Names: Kosann, Danielle, author. | Kosann, Laura, author. |
Pick, Aubrie, illustrator.
Title: Great tastes: Cooking (and eating) from morning
to midnight / by Danielle Kosann and Laura Kosann ;
photographs by Aubrie Pick.
Description: First edition. | New York: Clarkson Potter/
Publishers, 2018 | Includes index.
Identifiers: LCCN 2017026509| ISBN 9780553496376 |
ISBN 9780553496383 (ebook)
Subjects: LCSH: Cooking. | LCGFT: Cookbooks.
Classification: LCC TX714 .K658 2018 | DDC 641.5—
dc23 LC record available at https://lccn.loc.gov/2017026509.

ISBN 978-0-553-49637-6
Ebook ISBN 978-0-553-49638-3

Printed in China

Book and cover design by Ian Dingman
Cover photograph by Aubrie Pick

10 9 8 7 6 5 4 3 2 1

First Edition